The Wealth of Nations and the Environment

MIKHAIL S. BERNSTAM

Senior Research Fellow,
Hoover Institution, Stanford, California

Institute of Economic Affairs
1991

First published in January 1991

by

THE INSTITUTE OF ECONOMIC AFFAIRS

2 Lord North Street, Westminster, London SW1P 3LB

Occasional Paper 85

ISSN 0073-909X

ISBN 0-255 36240-4

The Institute gratefully acknowledges financial support for its publications programme and other work from a generous benefaction by the late Alec and Beryl Warren.

Printed in Great Britain by

GORON PRO-PRINT CO LTD, LANCING, WEST SUSSEX

Set in Berthold Plantin 11 on 12 point

Contents

[3]

FIGURES:

[5]

[6]

Foreword

SEVERAL YEARS ago it would have been difficult to gain acceptance for the claim that capitalism was more environmentally friendly than other economic systems. The reaction would have been one of almost universal disbelief – surely industry in capitalist economies puts profits before pretty well all else, resulting in accelerating environmental degradation! Intellectuals, the media and economists would have supplied many examples of the ills of capitalism. It would follow that a non-capitalist economy offers better safeguards for the environment. After all, if the State, the managers of state industries and the people said that they were interested in the social aspects of life – and lived in a society without the profit motive and private property – then it must follow that the environment would suffer less damage than that inflicted in a capitalist country. Few would make these claims today. The fall of the Iron Curtain has unveiled environmental devastation far exceeding the alleged excesses of present-day capitalist economies. The dismal economic performance of socialist and communist economies has been achieved at high costs to the environment, and the health of their citizens and workers.

Some may argue that this was accidental and/or transitional. Mikhail Bernstam is not content with such explanations. Rather he sees the divergence between the environmental record of capitalism and socialism as having its roots in the different structures of incentives and property rights of these two economic systems. Bernstam shows that the pursuit of profit in a capitalist economy leads to the husbanding of resources. Mature capitalist economies use fewer resources to produce the equivalent level of output and hence do less damage to the environment. Note here the green case for 'de-industrialisation'. In contrast, the managers of state enterprises operate under incentives that encourage them to maximise inputs, thus creating economic waste and continuing and increasing damage to the environment. There is no 'hidden hand' operating to limit and correct for environmental damage.

[7]

Bernstam offers his readers a cogent and subtly argued discussion of the relationships between economic growth, environmental problems and property rights. His *Occasional Paper* is rich in examples, evidence and analysis. Its conclusions will, I believe, surprise many, anger some, but challenge all. Although the views contained in this *Occasional Paper* are solely those of the author, the Institute commends it to all those concerned about the environment and economic growth.

December 1990   CENTO VELJANOVSKI

The Author

DR MIKHAIL S. BERNSTAM is a Senior Research Fellow at the Hoover Institution, Stanford University (since 1981). In 1989, he was Professor of Economics at Monash University in Melbourne. His latest publications (co-edited with Kingsley Davis) include *Below-Replacement Fertility in Industrial Societies: Causes, Consequences, Policies* (Cambridge University Press, 1987), *Population and Resources in a Changing World* (Stanford University, 1989), *Resources, Environment, and Population: Present Knowledge, Future Options* (Supplement to Vol. 16 of the journal *Population and Development Review*, 1990). He has also published numerous articles on the impact of the welfare state on population and is currently working on a book on the economic transition to free markets in socialist countries.

The Wealth of Nations and the Environment
MIKHAIL S. BERNSTAM

Introduction

DOES economic growth continuously and universally increase environmental disruption? Virtually all the economic literature answers in the affirmative.[1] This answer is damning for the wealth of nations, especially for those with low incomes.

Yet growing evidence shows that high levels of economic development and continuing economic growth in some countries, namely those with open competitive market economies, have recently reversed the relationship between expansion and pollution from positive to negative.[2] Smil and Kuz (1976) and Slade (1987, pp. 353-56) found a similar reversal in the relation between energy consumption *per capita* and GNP *per capita*. Winiecki (1983, 1987, pp. 16-26) showed that this reversal applies only to market economies; in socialist countries energy use continuously increases with or without economic growth.

This *Occasional Paper* will venture to show how, and explain why, the long-term relationship between economic growth and pollution may be inverse at higher levels of economic development. Simply put, as economies grow, discharges to the environment increase rapidly, then decelerate, and eventually decline. I will also analyse why this relationship exists for market economies but not for socialist ones.

The Framework

The first section surveys the evidence across nations with different economic systems. The second section discusses the

---

[1] Ayres and Kneese, 1969; Kneese, Ayres, d'Arge, 1970; US Commission on Population Growth and the American Future, 1972, pp. 43-49; Holdren and Ehrlich, 1974; Kneese, 1977, pp. 64-71, 84-89; Simon, 1981, p. 241; Slade, 1987, p. 339; Baumol and Oates, 1984, add several qualifications.

[2] Data in United Nations Environment Programme, 1987; OECD, 1989.

pattern of resource usage in different economies and stages of economic development. Its changes and the ensuing trends in pollution lie in a different dimension from the growth or decline of national incomes. In short, economic growth can be due to non-resource sectors (agriculture and services) and it can be due to technological progress which may either increase or reduce the input of resources and emission of pollutants. According to the law of conservation of mass, the weight of discharges to the environment resulting from production processes (including outputs that are used up over time) must be equal to the mass of resource inputs.[1] I discuss the trend in resource use as the race between growing (and then declining) resource-containing output and productivity of resource inputs in the production of this output. The outcome of this race, not economic growth, determines whether the total resource input and environmental discharges increase or decline.

The third section shows that the resulting trend in the pattern of resource use and pollution ultimately depends on the nature of the economic system. The two extreme systems, open competitive markets and regulated state monopolies, create different patterns of resource use.[2] I characterise these patterns as, respectively, cost minimisation and input maximisation. It is this systemic difference in resource use that leads to quite different environmental consequences in market and socialist economies.

The fourth section puts this divergence in the context of global economic development. Arithmetically, the future of the environment depends on the race between population growth and an improvement in the throughput of resources within the finite ecological niche. I therefore provide rough estimates of future environmental conditions according to different scenarios of the global choice of economic system.

1. The Tale of Two Industrial Developments

Prior to the iron age when coal was burnt to cast iron, most economic activity had little effect on the environment. Hunters and gatherers were only 'skimming the environment' (Davis,

[1] Kneese, Ayres, d'Arge, 1970; Haveman, 1974; Kneese, 1977; Hufschmidt et al., 1983; James, 1985; Forsund, 1985.
[2] Kornai, 1979, 1980, 1982, 1986a, 1986b; Winiecki, 1983, 1987.

1986, p. 63). Traditional agriculture derived its inputs from photosynthesis, not from physical resources, and thus did not produce atmospheric pollution (Ayres and Kneese, 1969; Kneese, Ayres, d'Arge, 1970, pp. 9, 32). At the same time, the cultivation of the woodlands and grasslands and the ensuing destruction of the forests affected the quality of the terrain. However, the main environmental impact of agriculture was the spread of livestock wastes. Although they were recycled, the process was inefficient, and water pollution was significant. High mortality from infectious diseases during this period supports this point. The use of animal power in agriculture, trade and transport increased livestock numbers and the ensuing pollution. Sea coal was burnt for home heating in the Middle Ages, and the extent of pollution led to the first recorded environmental policies. Already in 13th- and 14th-century England there was legislation which punished offenders (incidentally, by death) for the air pollution from coal burning, and navigation on the Thames was greatly impeded by human, horse, and early industrial wastes. The descriptions of carbonous air pollution in London in 1700 are as scary as those of Los Angeles in 1990 (Baumol and Oates, 1984, pp. 442-44). Mechanisation reduced pollution from horse wastes:

'When the automobile began to replace the horse and rid the streets of odorous dungheaps, it was hailed as a major contributor to public health and sanitation. Certainly the modern city, whatever its state of cleanliness, is an improvement on the relatively tiny, but incredibly filthy, streets and waterways of medieval and Renaissance cities.'[1]

Not only the modern city but also the modern countryside greatly improved its sources of drinking water and general sanitary conditions. This should be kept in mind against the increase in industrial sources of pollution.[2]

The Industrial Revolution and the Environment

The Industrial Revolution, itself a response to energy shortages, created a new environmental problem. Over the last two centuries, global levels of carbon dioxide in the air increased from 260-280 to 340 parts per million and the levels of nitrogen

[1] Baumol and Oates, 1984, p. 442.
[2] Simon (1981, pp. 131-43, 245) advances this point.

[13]

oxides from 281-291 to 304-310 parts per billion (United Nations Environment Programme, 1987, pp. 4, 9, 20). I have roughly calculated from the sketchy data that the amount of emissions of carbon dioxide has increased since the Industrial Revolution from 430 million metric tons (MMT) per year to 5,330 MMT in 1984.[1] This 12-fold increase is not remarkable. The remarkable fact is that world population increased from 1786 to 1986 by about 5·8 times (from 845 million to 4,917 million),[2] and the average GNP *per capita* increased probably 19 times.[3] The growth of the world economy from 1786 to 1986 was of the order of 110-fold against the 12-fold increase in global carbon dioxide.

Similar rough comparisons can be made for sulphur oxides and the world economy, nitrogen oxides and the world economy, and so on. The fundamental point is unambiguous. Contrary to the standard literature (e.g., Holdren and Ehrlich, 1974; Slade, 1987, p. 339), environmental discharges do not grow proportionately with the level of economic growth. More reliable data for this century in Western developed countries support this observation. For example, in the United States between 1940 and 1970, before major anti-pollution efforts were adopted, the total amount of emissions from major air pollutants increased by about 30 per cent. The real gross national product increased by some 212 per cent (US Bureau of the Census, 1989, pp. 200, 421).

The available long-term data suggest not only non-proportionality of pollution with respect to economic growth, but also that it eventually falls. The evidence strongly suggests that pollution levels grow at a decreasing rate and then fall increasingly during decades of rapid economic growth. Even when aggregate data for all countries is combined together for

[1] OECD, 1989, p. 45; United Nations Environment Programme, 1987, pp. 4, 9.

[2] Ronald D. Lee, 'Longrun Global Population Forecasts: A Critical Appraisal', in Kingsley Davis and Mikhail S. Bernstam (eds.), *Resources, Environment, and Population: Present Knowledge, Future Options*, Supplement to *Population and Development Review*, Vol. 16, 1990.

[3] I generously assume the average GNP per capita in 1786 as $150, on a par with today's Bangladesh, Mozambique, Nepal, and Zaire; GNP per capita in 1986 was $610 in developing countries, $6,740 in oil exporting countries, and $12,960 in industrial market countries (The World Bank, 1988, pp. 222-23). I also assume GNP *per capita* in developed socialist countries to be 40 per cent of that in market economies; this makes the average global GNP *per capita* in 1986 equal to $2,850 and the global GNP equal to $14 trillion.

countries in different stages of development and with different economic systems, they still show pollution levels falling with high levels of economic growth. This is true in the case of carbon dioxide and especially in global sulphur dioxide emissions data for the 125-year period, 1860-1985 (United Nations Environment Programme, 1987, pp. 7-8, 12). The average decadal rate of global increase of sulphur dioxide discharges was between 51 and 56 per cent over the 50 years 1860-1910, and between 8 and 21 per cent over 1910-50. The rate rose to between 28 and 32 per cent in 1950-80, with the peak of 39 per cent in the decade 1955-65. But the most dramatic changes occurred after 1970 for all major sources of air and water pollution throughout all Western market economies.

The Recent Environmental Split

In the 1970s and the 1980s, an amazing divergence took place in the trends in resource use and pollution within the developed industrial world. This divergence between Western market economies and the socialist economies of the USSR and Eastern Europe went virtually unnoticed. Yet, it may have signified the most important reversal in economic and environmental history since the Industrial Revolution. Tables 1-6 and Figure 1 summarise these trends for all economic systems. The amounts of throughput of major resources and the ensuing discharges of air, water, and soil pollution began to decline rapidly in those nations with competitive market economies. This is true notwithstanding further economic growth in Western market countries. During the same two decades, the throughput of resources and environmental disruption was rapidly increasing in the USSR and European socialist countries even though their economies slowed down and eventually stagnated.[1] Only a small fraction of the evidence can be surveyed here. The sources cited contain more data; I have also compiled some 600 less accessible Soviet sources.[2]

Table 1 shows emissions of major air pollutants in the United States in selected years from 1940 to 1986. Table 2 provides air pollution data for nine Western market economies during the period 1970-85. All emissions are broken down by sources,

[1] Gzovskii (1985) pointed out this apparent paradox.

[2] These sources are in my files and are available for examination on request.

[Contd. on p. 18]

Table 1

Air Pollutant Emissions, by Source and Types of Pollutant, in million metric tons: USA, Selected Years, 1940 to 1986

Year	Total	Sources		Emissions from all Sources				
		Transportation	Stationary* Sources	Particulate Matter	Sulphur Oxides	Nitrogen Oxides	Carbon Monoxide	Lead (thousand tons)
1940	147.1	n.a.	n.a.	22.8	17.5	6.8	81.6	n.a.
1960	165.4	n.a.	n.a.	21.1	19.5	12.8	88.4	n.a.
1970	191.4	93.8	76.0	18.5	28.4	18.1	98.7	203.8
1975	159.6	83.1	63.7	10.6	26.0	19.1	81.0	147.0
1980	151.9	72.3	64.6	8.5	23.9	20.3	76.1	70.6
1986	127.7	59.9	57.1	6.8	21.2	19.3	60.9	8.6

Notes:
*Stationary fuel combustion and industrial processes.

The data for sources of discharges do not add to the total in Table 1 because emissions from solid wastes and miscellaneous uncontrolled sources are not included. Table 2, by contrast, calculates the data from the OECD publication which uses a (perhaps illegitimate) broad definition of stationary sources inclusive of solid wastes and miscellaneous sources.

Sources: US Bureau of the Census, *Statistical Abstract of the United States, 1988*, Washington DC: US Government Printing Office, 1987, p. 192; US National Center for Health Statistics, *Health, United States, 1988*, Washington DC: US Government Printing Office, 1989, p. 103.

Table 2

Trends in Emissions of Air Pollutants in Market Economies, by Source: Selected Countries, 1970 to 1985, in thousand metric tons

	1970			1975			1980			1985			Ratio: 1985/1970 in per cent		
	A	S	T	A	S	T	A	S	T	A	S	T	A	S	T
Canada	10,078	12,068	22,146	10,619	11,089	21,708	9,975	10,552	20,527	9,340	10,260	19,600	92.7	85.0	88.5
USA	93,600	96,700	190,300	83,100	76,400	159,500	72,200	79,600	151,800	63,000	70,000	133,000	67.3	72.4	69.9
Germany	11,189	12,858	24,047	12,802	9,427	22,229	11,822	9,190	21,012	9,379	7,641	17,020	83.8	59.4	70.8
France	5,451	7,889	13,340	5,805	8,184	13,989	6,472	7,976	14,448	6,882*	4,830*	11,712*	126.3*	61.2*	87.8*
UK	4,395	11,435	15,830	4,942	9,547	14,489	5,722	8,908	14,630	5,636	7,574	13,210	128.2	66.2	83.4
Italy	6,590	5,552	12,142	6,680	4,633	11,313	6,666	4,699	11,365	6,674	3,511	10,185	101.3	63.2	83.9
Norway	n.a.	n.a.	n.a.	671	402	1,073	712	436	1,148	736	382	1,118	n.a.	n.a.	n.a.
Sweden	1,997	1,397	3,394	1,853	1,139	2,992	1,690	960	2,650	1,921	1,021	2,942	96.2	73.1	86.7
Netherlands	2,096	1,822	3,918	2,097	1,342	3,439	1,673	1,447	3,120	1,417	1,280	2,697	67.6	70.3	68.8

Notes:

A = emissions from transportation.
S = emissions from stationary sources.
T = total emissions.

*1987

In some cases, the data are missing on emissions from one of the five major emission sources in a given year. The data for a previous or subsequent year were then added assuming no change for a given source of emissions over a five-year period.

The data for sources of discharges do not add to the total in Table 1 because emissions from solid wastes and miscellaneous uncontrolled sources are not included. Table 2, by contrast, calculates the data from the OECD publication which uses a (perhaps illegitimate) broad definition of stationary sources inclusive of solid wastes and miscellaneous sources.

Source: Calculated from OECD, *OECD Environmental Data Compendium, 1989,* Paris: OECD, 1989, pp. 21–29.

mainly transport and stationary sources. The latter consist of discharges from fuel combustion and industrial processes. One can observe a very rapid decline in pollution in the 1970s and the 1980s, ranging from 12 per cent to 33 per cent depending on the country. The decline was so significant that, in the United States, emissions of 128 million metric tons in 1986 were 13 per cent lower than in 1940, although the US population rose by 82 per cent and the real gross national product increased by more than 380 per cent over the same period. Annual amounts of emissions decreased so steeply in the USA that even absolute levels of accumulated concentration of pollutants in the air began to decline after 1977.[1]

In addition to these spectacular falls in pollution levels, seven features stand out from the data which I have examined.

○ *First,* the decline in pollution occurred in many developed market economies of Europe and North America. The data for Japan is too sketchy but points in the same direction.

○ *Second,* the decline of emissions occurred in both transport and stationary sources and was often even more pronounced in the latter. Therefore, the hypothesis that the decline was due solely to a higher fuel-efficiency of cars is not supported by the evidence.

○ *Third,* declines in pollution occurred across most physical-chemical substances, not only those from fossil fuel sources. Therefore, the energy crisis of the 1970s and the 1980s cannot have been solely responsible.

○ *Fourth,* the extent of the government environmental regulation and environmentalist movements across countries does not correlate with the steepness of pollution declines. If anything, there is a slight negative correlation.

○ *Fifth,* the decline in pollution in the United States was faster in the 1980s than in the 1970s while economic growth was about the same (US Bureau of the Census, 1989, p. 421; Table 1).

○ *Sixth,* in the United States economic growth was roughly the same as in Western Europe in the 1970s but about twice as

[1] US Bureau of the Census, 1989, pp. 7, 421, 200.

[18]

high in the 1980s (US President, 1987, p. 368). But the USA experienced a more rapid decrease in pollution than most Western European nations. The latter two points suggest that the newly emerging negative relationship between economic growth and pollution may be accelerating.

o The final, *seventh* point will be examined later. This concerns the question of whether pollution abatement efforts in market countries were mainly responsible for the decline of emissions in the 1970s and the 1980s. A different hypothesis will emphasise a secular increase in the productivity of resource use in Western market economies which eventually produced absolute declines in resource throughput and pollution. These hypotheses are complementary in the high-income economies, but I want to emphasise the second phenomenon which is ignored in the environmental literature.

The decline in air pollution outlined above represents a part of a larger picture. It was accompanied in many market countries by similar noticeable improvements in water quality,[1] and reductions in pesticide residues in food, water and human bodies. There were even decreases in solid wastes, especially industrial wastes dumped at sea (United Nations Environment Programme, 1987, pp. 279, 284-89). Table 3 shows major reductions in pesticide residue in human tissue in the UK in 1963-83 and especially in the USA in 1970-83. Later in the paper I will relate such trends to growing productivity of inputs and their decreasing absolute use; meanwhile, one can consult the data on the trend in pesticides consumption. Since the mid-1970s, this consumption has significantly declined in the United States, Japan, Scandinavian countries, but only for one type of pesticides in the UK (US Bureau of the Census, 1989, p. 203; OECD, 1989, p. 299). The improvements in human exposure probably resulted from both the decrease of total use of pesticides and changes in the mix and impact of chemicals. Table 3 also compares human exposure to pesticides in 1979-82 across several Western market countries and in China and India, where pesticide residues in human milk are much higher while agricultural output *per capita* is much lower.

[1] US Bureau of the Census, 1989, p. 191; United Nations Environment Programme, 1987, pp. 37, 52, 56-59; OECD, 1987, pp. 61-67.

Table 3

Pesticide Residue Levels in Human Adipose Tissue and Human Milk: Selected Countries, 1963 to 1983, in mg per kg

	DDE	DDT	HCH (BHC)	Dieldrin
Human Tissue:				
UK				
1963–64	2.2	1.20	n.a.	0.27
1965–67	2.2	0.83	0.28	0.23
1969–71	1.9	0.54	0.27	0.16
1976–77	2.1	0.20	0.30	0.11
1982–83	1.3	0.01	0.24	0.07
USA				
1970		7.95*	0.37	0.16
1973		5.96*	0.25	0.17
1976		4.34*	0.18	0.09
1979		3.10*	0.15	0.08
1981		2.38*	0.10	0.05
1983		1.63*	0.08	0.06
Human Milk				
USA, 1979	2.0	0.10	0.05	n.a.
Japan, 1980–81	1.8	0.21	2.30	n.a.
West Germany, 1981	1.2	0.28	0.30	n.a.
Sweden, 1981	0.96	0.10	0.09	n.a.
Belgium, 1982	1.0	0.13	0.20	n.a.
Israel, 1981–82	2.4	0.26	0.37	n.a.
China, 1982	4.4	1.80	6.70	n.a.
India, 1982	5.4	1.20	4.70	n.a.

n.a.: not available
*Combined data for DDE and DDT.

Source: UN Environment Programme, *Environmental Data Report*, London: Basil Blackwell, 1987, pp. 100–101.

1970s and 1980s Pollution Growth in Socialist Countries

In contrast with the rapid decline in pollution in market economies, environmental disruption significantly increased in the 1970s and the 1980s in socialist countries.[1] Rapid environmental degradation includes rising air pollution and

---

[1] Li documents such trends for the People's Republic of China (see Jing-Neng Li, 'The Effects of Population Growth on Deforestation and Soil Erosion in China', in Davis and Bernstam, 1990; see also Smil, 1984).

[20]

increases in water pollution and soil erosion.[1] Discharges of polluted water increased in the USSR from 35 billion cubic metres in 1970 to 150 billion in 1988; the asserted abatement is 60-80 per cent ineffective (Lukianenko, 1989).

Two specific observations are relevant for relating trends in pollution to the analysis of economic systems. First, since 1985, the new Soviet administration began to change the USSR's economic system. Some of the most polluting plants were shut down. Air pollution has dropped by about 10 per cent during the last several years (USSR State Committee on Statistics, 1989a). Second, international data document increases in emissions and concentration of pollutants in Poland, Hungary, and Czechoslovakia, but, curiously, the trends are mixed in Yugoslavia.[2] Yugoslavia modified its socialist economic system, and its monopolistic enterprises do not have to maximise inputs in order to maximise profits, justify price increases, and relax output quotas.

Estimates of emissions of air pollutants in socialist countries are deficient because about 76-80 per cent of discharges from stationary sources are assumed to be abated according to nominal technical capabilities of scrubbers and precipitators. But actual abatement does not exceed 30 per cent (compare USSR State Committee on Statistics, 1989b, p. 249, with Lisovenko and Trach, 1989, Tsaturov, 1989, and Simons, 1990). Due to this uncertainty about the data, I assume as the lower bound the amount of emissions in socialist countries at the 77 per cent level of abatement from stationary sources. The amount at the 30 per cent of abatement ratio from stationary sources is assumed to be the higher bound of pollution.

No adjustments are made for air pollution from transport. In the USSR in 1988, emissions from transport were estimated to amount to 35·6 million metric tonnes (Valentei, 1990) against 59·9 MMT in the United States in 1986. There were 71 land vehicles of all types per 1,000 persons in the USSR and 723 in the USA (calculated from US Bureau of the Census, 1989, p. 825). Given the differences in population size, emissions per

[1] For example, USSR Supreme Soviet, 1989; Iablokov, 1989; USSR State Committee on Statistics, 1989a; Samsonov, 1989; Voloshin, 1990.

[2] United Nations Environment Programme, 1987, pp. 13, 15; OECD, 1989, pp. 21, 61-63.

Table 4

Pollutant Emissions from Stationary Sources, in million metric tons: USA, 1986, and USSR, 1987

	USA	USSR
Total	57.1	64.1
Particulate Matter	4.3	15.6
Sulphur Oxides	20.3	18.6
Nitrogen Oxides	10.6	4.5
Carbon Monoxide	11.7	15.5
Volatile Organic Compounds	10.2	9.9

Sources: USA: US National Center for Health Statistics, *Health, United States, 1988,* Washington DC: US Government Printing Office, 1989, p. 103.
USSR: USSR State Committee on Statistics, *Narodnoe Khoziaistvo SSSR v 1987 Godu,* Moscow, 1988, p. 571.

vehicle were nine times as high in the USSR as in the USA; the gap would widen if airplanes were included. The total amount of Soviet air pollution from transport is thus relatively small because there are few cars and trucks.

Table 4 compares the US and USSR emissions of air pollutants from stationary sources in the mid-1980s. The lower estimates of the Soviet data are used. Using this conservative assumption, Soviet levels of emissions are higher than American ones. The higher estimate of Soviet emissions of air pollutants from stationary sources can be calculated for 1987 as 275·7 MMT (USSR State Committee on Statistics, 1988, p. 571). This is 4·8 times higher than in the USA while the Soviet GNP is *less than half as high.* Using the above numbers and the OECD data from Table 2 and related sources for two groups of countries, I roughly estimated air pollution from both transport and stationary sources in market and socialist economies. At the lower bound, the amount of discharges of air pollutants *per capita* in socialist countries is approximately the same as in Western market economies, about 350 kilograms (kg) per year. This is at the level of GNP *per capita* in socialist countries about 40 per cent of that in Western market economies (Illarionov, 1990, pp. 6-7). At the higher bound, the socialist average is 800 kg *per capita,* that is, 2·3 times higher than in market economies. The ratios per $1,000 of GNP in socialist versus market economies are much higher: 2·5 times at the lower bound and 5·8 times at the higher bound.

[22]

Comparative Trends in Resource Use

My explanation of the environmental divergence within the developed industrial world is simple. It is due to different patterns of resource use. First, resource use per unit of output is much higher in socialist than in market economies. On a *per capita* basis, resource use in socialist countries is as high as or higher than in the West, although socialist GNP *per capita* is about 40 per cent of that in Western market countries.[1] Second, inputs of basic resources declined in Western market economies during the last two decades of economic growth and technological progress. These inputs continuously increased in socialist economies with or without economic growth.

Tables 5 and 6 and Figure 1 present comparative trends in resource inputs with the special emphasis on energy. This emphasis here and throughout the paper is warranted because in industrial societies energy conversion constitutes about 50 per cent of total resource use (Haveman, 1974, p. 103). Table 5 and Figure 1 show that, measured by energy consumption *per capita*, the USSR has been converging with the USA, and socialist economies in general have been converging with market economies in general. They have been converging exactly because the trends have been diverging: the downward trend in market economies and the upward trend in socialist economies. *Per capita* energy consumption in the USA and Canada in the 1980s was only slightly higher than in 1960. In the 1970s and 1980s, energy consumption *per capita* declined in most Western economies. In absolute terms, which are ultimately important for environmental discharges, total consumption of energy declined in the 1980s in the United States, Canada, West Germany, France, Sweden and Belgium, and remained stable in Japan, Italy, the Netherlands, Denmark, and Austria. At the same time, total energy consumption increased significantly in the USSR (by about 25 per cent) and most other socialist countries.[2]

Similar divergent trends led to the widening of the gap in *per capita* steel consumption in market and socialist economies in the 1970s and the 1980s (Table 5). In terms of both energy and steel, the ratio of inputs per $1,000 of GNP in socialist and

[1] New semi-official Soviet estimates of GNP *per capita* are in Illarionov, 1990.
[2] See OECD, 1989, p. 235; US Bureau of the Census, 1989, pp. 833-34; United Nations Environment Programme, 1987, pp. 256-89.   [*Contd. on p. 26*]

Table 5
Consumption of Energy and Steel per capita and per $1,000 of GNP: Selected Countries, 1975, 1980 and 1985–86

	Energy (in kilograms of coal equivalent)				Steel (in metric tons)			
	Per Capita		Per $1,000 of GNP*		Per Capita		Per $1,000 of GNP*	
	1980	1986	1980	1986	1975	1985	1975	1985
Market Economies								
USA	10,386	9,489	690	590	541	448	40	28
Canada	10,547	9,694	840	740	581	471	51	35
Japan	3,726	3,625	410	330	580	553	78	51
UK	4,850	5,363	670	680	376	254	56	32
West Germany	5,829	5,672	600	550	489	481	60	47
France	4,409	3,881	500	430	365	258	48	29
Belgium	5,997	5,577	780	710	314	275	48	36
Switzerland	3,636	3,990	250	260	n.a.	n.a.	n.a.	n.a.
Austria	4,058	4,024	500	460	284	235	44	27
Denmark	5,254	5,331	340	290	n.a.	n.a.	n.a.	n.a.
Sweden	5,376	4,893	500	430	773	384	75	34
South Korea	1,373	1,625	870	790	52	198**	42	93**
Unweighted average	5,450	5,260	580	520	436	356	54	41
Socialist Economies								
USSR	5,549	6,389	1,130	1,250	554	557	124	121
Bulgaria	5,254	5,780	1,310	1,590	252	336	64	80
Czechoslovakia	6,364	6,258	1,160	1,100	731	709	144	124
East Germany	7,276	7,944	1,150	1,920	566	574	101	82
Hungary	3,787	3,735	800	760	n.a.	n.a.	n.a.	n.a.
Poland	4,935	4,700	1,150	1,100	524	409	120	95
Romania	4,505	4,483	1,340	1,260	463	480	159	133
North Korea	2,713	2,771	2,490	2,450	186	413	177	356
Unweighted average	5,048	5,260	1,320	1,430	468	497	127	142

*In constant 1984 dollars. Estimates per $1,000 of GNP in socialist countries are corrected assuming the average GNP *per capita* in these countries equal to 40% of that in Western market economies (for recent semi-official Soviet estimates, see A. Illarionov, 'Paradoksy Statistiki', *Argumenty i Fakty*, No. 3, 1990, pp. 6–7). No corrections were made for North Korea due to lack of data.

**1984.   n.a.: not available.

Source: US Bureau of the Census, *Statistical Abstract of the United States, 1989*, Washington DC: USGPO, 1989, pp. 822, 832–34.

Table 6
Comparable Data on Trends in Productive Activities: USA and USSR, 1960, 1970, and 1987

	USA			USSR		
	1960	1970	1987	1960	1970	1987
Oil and Gas Condensate (million tons)	348	475	415	148	353	624
Natural Gas (billion cubic metres)	n.a.	621	480	n.a.	200	678
Coal (million tons)	400	542	820	371	577	680
Electricity (trillion W/hr)	892	1,730	2,750	292	740	1,665
Electricity for Industrial Use (trillion W/hr)	n.a.	730	870	n.a.	488	957
Iron Ore (million tons)[a]	89	90.7	36	106	195	251
Pig Iron (million tons)[a]	n.a.	83.3	44	n.a.	85.9	114
Steel (million tons)[a]	92	122	81	65	116	162
Cement (million tons)	56.1	66.5	81.6	45.5	95.2	137
Chemicals (thousand tons)	774	2,250	4,100	211	623	1,517
Synthetics and Plastics (million tons)	2.9	n.a.	25.5	0.29	n.a.	4.5
Tractors (thousands)	n.a.	224	93	n.a.	459	567
Grain Combines (thousands)	n.a.	24.0	8.3	n.a.	99.2	96.2
Mineral Fertilizers (million nutrient tons)	7.6	14.9	20.0	3.3	13.1	36.3
Pesticides (thousand tons of active mass)[b]	n.a.	342	236	n.a.	264	328
Grain (million tons)	147.6[c]	168.2[c]	280.9[c]	125.5[d]	186.7[d]	211.4[d]
Cattle (million head)	97.7	112.4	102.0	75.8	95.1	120.9
Hogs and Pigs (million head)	59.0	57.0	51.0	58.7	56.1	79.5
Meat, Carcass Weight (million tons)	18.6	23.8	28.9	8.7[d]	12.3[d]	18.9[d]
Milk Cows (million head)	19.5	13.3	10.5	34.8	40.5	42.4
Milk per Cow (tons)	2.9	4.4	6.0	1.8	2.1	2.7

[a] Domestic production. Net of exports and imports, domestic consumption of iron ore in 1986 was 51.8 million metric tons (MMT) in the USA and 214.0 MMT in the USSR. Consumption of pig iron was 48.5 MMT and 108.5 MMT, respectively. Consumption of steel was 99.2 MMT in the USA and 160.6 MMT in the USSR.

[b] Annual averages for 1976–1980 and 1981–1985 are presented in columns for 1970 and 1987, respectively. The definition in the Soviet source and thus the measurement are not clear; US sources provide different numbers but for US only; the data are presented here only for comparative purpose.

[c] Sorghum, barley and rice are not included. The totals are about 12% higher if these are included.

[d] To convert to international definitions, this gross amount should be higher by at least 15%.

Sources: USSR Central Statistical Department, *Narodnoe Khoziaistvo SSSR v 1970 godu. Statisticheskii Ezhegodnik*, Moscow, 1971, pp. 94–97, 352, 367; USSR State Committee on Statistics, *Narodnoe Khoziaistvo SSSR v 1987 godu. Statisticheskii Ezhegodnik*, Moscow, 1988, pp. 123–24, 126, 213, 226, 603–604, 633–45; US Bureau of the Census, *Statistical Abstract of the United States, 1961*, Washington DC: USGPO, 1961, pp. 651–52, 676–77, 681; US Bureau of the Census, *Statistical Abstract of the United States, 1981*, Washington DC: USGPO, 1981, pp. 686, 688–89, 693; *Statistical Abstract of the United States, 1988*, Washington DC: USGPO, 1987, pp. 633–35; *Statistical Abstract of the United States, 1989*, Washington DC: USGPO, 1989, pp. 643, 686, 740–41, 832. Pesticides: Boris Cherniakov, 'Khimiia iii Zhizn', *Moscow News*, No. 25, June 1989, p. 10.

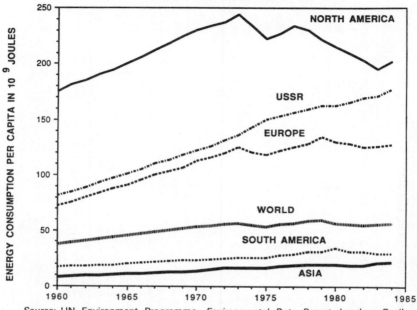

Figure 1
Energy Consumption Per Capita
by Selected World Regions, 1960-84

NORTH AMERICA

USSR

EUROPE

WORLD

SOUTH AMERICA

ASIA

ENERGY CONSUMPTION PER CAPITA IN 10⁹ JOULES

Source: UN Environment Programme, *Environmental Data Report*, London: Basil Blackwell, 1987, p. 247.

market economies increased from about 2·5:1 in the second half of the 1970s to about 3:1 in the mid-1980s. The gap is wider between the USSR and the USA. Given low population growth in Western countries, one can readily infer from Table 5 that steel consumption declined there in absolute terms. The same is true for many other primary metals. Table 5 permits comparisons to be made between East Germany and West Germany and between North Korea and South Korea. In both cases, the differences in resource use per $1,000 of GNP and *per capita* were either the same or even more pronounced than between the two groups of countries on the average.

Table 6 provides a broader picture comparing the resource throughput (resource use from inputs to outputs) in the Soviet Union and the United States in 1960, 1970, and 1987 over the chains of production processes. It is worth noting that the decline in domestic production of resources and materials in the United States as presented in Table 6 is generally larger than the decline in their consumption which includes imports. The direction of both trends is, however, the same.[1] For environmental analysis, total consumption of energy is more relevant than domestic production, but domestic production of metals is as relevant as final consumption. It is domestic processing of ores into primary and fabricated metals (e.g., forging steel) that generates environmental damage. When primary and fabricated metals are imported, some part of domestic pollution is in effect exported by more developed to newly industrialised countries.

Long-term decline in US use of energy and other resources

Table 6 shows that there has been a very dramatic decline in the use of many physical resources in the United States between 1970 and 1987 after a significant increase in the 1960s. This reversal of the trend closely corresponds to a similar reversal in the trend in pollution presented in Table 1. This suggests that the decline in discharges was not due predominantly to abatement efforts. The effect was largely produced by the decline of resource and material inputs per unit of output in production chains (for example, more meat with fewer heads of livestock and with less feed grain with fewer tractors and combines out of less steel from less pig iron out of less iron ore). This reduced the discharge of pollution.

Actually, this was a continuation of the long-term trend in the reduction of resource inputs per unit of GNP – the declining trend which had been for decades overshadowed by the growth of resource content within the GNP. In the USA, energy consumption per $1,000 of GNP has been steadily declining at 1 per cent per year for 60 years from 1929 to 1989. In 1989 it was about 55 per cent of the 1929 level; Japan has had a similar trend since the 1950s (Yoichi, Kenju, and Ryuji, 1989). In the 1970s and the 1980s, the production of both coal and electricity continued to increase in the USA, but productivity of electricity in terms of coal usage increased even more. The share of electricity for industrial use as a proportion of the total consumption of electricity declined by about 25 per cent (Table 6).

Table 6 also shows the decline in the total amount of inputs

[1] See US Bureau of the Census, 1989, pp. 679-80, 686, 740-41; and Table 5 and Figure 1.

[27]

after 1970 in the United States. What began as the decline in the amount of resources used to produce $1,000 of GNP, continued as the decline *per capita* and eventually resulted in an absolute decline in the total consumption of resources. This encompasses oil and gas, iron ore and iron-originated materials and outputs, and the stock of farm animals. The latter is especially important in the context of water pollution. In the 1970s and the 1980s there were fewer machines and fertilisers per ton of grain, less grain per ton of meat, fewer cattle and swine per ton of meat and fewer cows per ton of milk, just as there was less pig iron and cotton. Most of these trends accelerated during these two decades. For example, in the 1970s, the total physical volume of all mining products in the USA increased slightly and the production of all primary metals declined by 5 per cent. They both declined by 10 per cent in the 1980s (US Bureau of the Census, 1989, p. 730). In short, major improvements in resource productivity and the corresponding reductions in resource inputs occurred throughout the US economy.

Table 6 also shows that the Soviet trends have been in reverse of the American ones. All major physical resource-using inputs and outputs have expanded in the 1970s and the 1980s in continuing the trend of the 1960s. With the exception of coal, all inputs expanded either much faster than in the USA or rapidly increased when analogous production in the USA declined sharply. Soviet production of oil, gas, steel, cement, fertilisers and pesticides, agricultural machinery, and the number of cattle and swine, often starting from levels lower than those in the United States in 1960, exceeded that of the USA by 1987 – with little positive benefit to the consumer economy, and with dire environmental costs.

Continuous increases in resource use in USSR
Even the advantage of economic backwardness, widely discussed in the literature on Japan's and other countries' economic development, when a nation can easily leap upward from low output levels by using proven Western technology, does not seem to help in the Soviet case. Consider milk yield per cow. It obviously has some biological limits, and there must be diminishing increases with rising yield. Yet it doubled in the USA in 27 years from a level in 1960 which the USSR had not achieved by 1987, while the Soviet increase over the same period

was only 50 per cent. Over the entire production chains from final products to raw materials in the USSR, there were continuous increases in resource use, which explains the continuous rise in environmental damage. Table 5 and other related evidence suggests that this conclusion applies to all socialist countries and their economic systems.

2. The Race Between Productivity of Resources and Population Growth

The evidence so far shows that economic growth and environmental disruption do not necessarily go hand in glove. Pollution can decline or increase when the economy grows and it can increase when the economy does not grow. What it will do depends crucially on the incentives structure of the economy. The following section will present a simple accounting mechanism which explains these relationships.

Introducing the Race Between Resource Productivity and Resource Output

Consider both separate and overlapping systems of economic and material accounting sketched in Figure 2. According to the law of conservation of mass, the total amount of discharges of residuals to the environment (including outputs that are used over time) is equal to the weight of inputs of resources (including oxygen derived from the atmosphere and alloyed during processing [Ayres and Kneese, 1969, pp. 284-85]). This is shown at the bottom of Figure 2. The amount of pollution is smaller than the weight of residuals. Not all residuals are pollutants, and some potential pollutants are abated and/or recycled. Weight, however, is not the only parameter of pollution. Highly toxic pollutants, radiation, etc., significantly affect the environment and people, but do not weigh much. This requires attention in any empirical analysis. At the moment, we need to separate, distinguish, and disaggregate economic and material balances on the top and in the centre of Figure 2. The economy has two dimensions: the economic product ('gross national product') and the material product (physical throughput).

The gross national product consists of both resource-using output and non-resource output. The latter consists of agricultural

Figure 2
Economic and Material Accounting

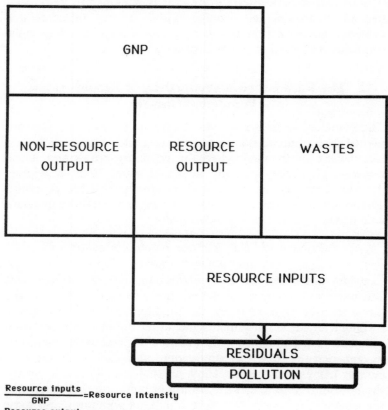

$$\frac{\text{Resource inputs}}{\text{GNP}} = \text{Resource Intensity}$$

$$\frac{\text{Resource output}}{\text{Resource inputs}} = \text{Resource Productivity}$$

products of photosynthesis and various services including engineering. The material throughput of the economy has total resource inputs (or total resource use) at the beginning of production and two types of production at the end. One type of final production is the resource-using output which has economic value. This is identical with the resource part of the GNP. The other part is everything else that derives from resources, has no economic value and/or serves no useful purpose. These are uselessly processed resources, or wastes (in an economic, not a

[30]

physical sense; 'waste' in the physical sense usually denotes all residuals, including outputs that are used up). Resource output plus resource wastes are the total resource use. The previous three sentences hold the key to the entire argument of this paper and, if this argument is correct, to the entire relationship between economic growth and environmental disruption.

For it is the change in the amount of these wastefully used resources that determines the relationship between economic growth and pollution. Wastes, such as scrap, spills, slag, discards, refuses, and other processing losses (Ayres and Kneese, 1969, pp. 283-85; Kneese, Ayres, d'Arge, 1970, p. 9), do not contribute to real economic well-being. Wastes also include destroyed primary resources (for instance, Amazonian rain forests felled and burnt in order to clear pasture land for livestock production) and losses of intermediary and final output in transport and storage (for example, losses of agricultural output which range from 20 to 40 per cent in the Soviet Union).[1] According to estimates made at the USSR Central Institute of Mathematical Economics, about 33 per cent of industrial production is economically useless output, mostly unnecessary and unutilised producer goods and various primary and intermediary outputs involved in the production of this machinery (Uliukaev, 1989, p. 84; Aganbegian, 1987).

When the technical efficiency of resource use grows, wastes and input/output ratios decline over the production cycle. Inversely, productivity of resources, defined as the ratio of economically useful resource outputs to total resource inputs, increases. If the productivity of resources increases faster (that is, the amount of resource wastes declines faster) than resource output increases, then the total amount of resource inputs declines. Resource output may grow, as it did ever since the Industrial Revolution, and thus make the GNP grow, but resource use and pollution may decline. Economic growth and pollution decline occur simultaneously. This becomes possible for the same technological reason: the growth in resource productivity in excess of the growth of resource output.

One can conduct a visual experiment and imagine these changes on Figure 2. Simply increase resource output and thus

[1] According to the USSR State Committee on Statistics, 1989c, p. 13; Rimashevskaia, 1990, p. 35.

[31]

the GNP by a square unit but reduce wastes by, say, 1·5 square units. Resource inputs and pollution are reduced by 0·5 square units while the GNP is increased by 1 square unit. The growth in resource productivity outpaced the growth in resource output. The race is won, and pollution declined. Economic growth actually reduced pollution. This is what has happened in Western market economies in the 1970s and the 1980s.

Figure 2 also shows that non-polluting economic growth is possible due to the non-resource sector. In this case, resource intensity (inputs per unit of GNP) declines and resource use and pollution remain unchanged. Pollution and resource inputs decline only if resource intensity declines faster than GNP grows, that is, if the efficiency improvements described above take place in the resource sector. The decisive race is the race against wastes, the race between resource output and resource productivity. There is also one more participant in the race, on whom the absolute amount of resource output depends: that is, population.

Environmental Damage as the Outcome of the Race Between Productivity and Population

At each given level of resource output *per capita* and resource productivity, the size of population determines the absolute amount of resource use and eventual discharges to the environment. All other things being equal, more people means more resource use, and higher productivity of resources means lower resource use. The ultimate race, therefore, is between population growth and the growth of resource productivity. This is established technically in Appendix A (below, pp. 61-62).

Holdren and Ehrlich (1974) proposed a measure of environmental damage which is defined as the product of three multipliers: population size, consumption *per capita*, and environmental pollution per unit of consumption. However, this formula is misleading. The use of consumption *per capita* for measuring pollution is a misnomer, unless consumption is defined as the total resource use – that is, all production minus non-resource-using consumption. Otherwise, the Holdren-Ehrlich formula violates the law of conservation of mass. From the wrong definition of the central multiplier and from the extension of the static accounting formula to a dynamic relationship, the

[32]

standard inference is derived that economic growth increases pollution.

Here I present different formulae which satisfy the law of conservation of mass in Appendix A.

In simple terms, environmental damage is caused by the total amount of resource-using outputs, including economically useful output and various wastes. By the law of conservation of mass, this total amount is identical to the total amount of resource inputs. The resulting damage to the environment is also identical. In this context, one can incorporate the notion of resource productivity defined as the ratio of economically useful resource-related output to the total amount of resource inputs. The inverse of resource productivity is the ratio of resource inputs to useful output. By extension, the total amount of resource inputs can now be thought of as the product of useful output and the input/useful output ratio. Accordingly, environmental damage is caused by the product of useful output and input/useful output ratios. It directly follows that environmental damage may decline if input/useful output ratios decline faster than the amount of useful output increases. In other words, environmental damage may decline if resource productivity increases faster than the growth of resource-using, economically useful output. In this sense, the quality of the environment depends on the outcome of the race between the two principal multipliers, namely, resource-using output and the productivity of resources.

It also follows that when useful output is measured on a *per capita* basis and the environmental damage is thus dependent on population size, there is a race between resource productivity and population growth. In all cases, the growth of resource productivity (or, inversely, the reduction of input/useful output ratios or the reduction of wastes) has been a crucial factor in the history of the relations between man and nature.

Resource output *per capita*, as one component of the level of economic well-being, cannot solely, by itself, determine the level and the course of pollution. Even less so can the level of income *per capita* which is outside the material balance. The direct dynamic inference is that economic growth can increase pollution if it increases the resource output of the economy; and economic growth can reduce pollution if it increases the

[33]

productivity of resources (that is, reduces wastes) faster than both resource output and population growth.

From hunting and gathering to agriculture to industry, output has included an increasing proportion of natural resources. Many new resources were involved in production. The productivity of new resources, be they livestock or fossil fuels or metals, is initially low. The average resource productivity thus declines while the amount of both resource outputs and wastes grows. New resources bring to the scene new environmental damages and increase the average unit damage. Even without population growth, the agricultural and then especially industrial development increases environmental damage multifold. Population growth merely magnifies this effect. This expansion of resource usage, rather than economic growth *per se*, is at the core of the damage explosion of the industrial era.

Then the process decelerates; productivity of resources and resource output *per capita* compete. As long as the latter outpaces the former, which was characteristic of industrial development until recent reversal in Western market economies, total resource use, its total residuals, and their pollution increase. The latter three increase more and more slowly as the growth of productivity of resources catches up with the growth of resource output. Again, population growth magnifies the increase in residuals. Later, population growth cancels in absolute terms the improvements on a *per capita* basis when productivity of resources outpaces the growth of useful output *per capita*, and the resource use *per capita* declines. The process decelerates more and more until the point is reached at which resource output *per capita* grows more slowly than resource productivity or not at all, while resource productivity grows faster than population. Then the concave curve of pollution goes down, as was documented earlier (above, pp. 27-28).

Damage per unit of mass of resources is another participant in this multivariate race. Total damage depends, among other things, on resource mix. Additions of new resources to processing at early industrial stages worsen the mix in environmental terms. Further substitution of new materials (for instance, fibre optics for copper) reduces both the mass of inputs per unit of output and environmental damage per unit of mass. Improvements in resource mix are a powerful reducer of pollution. Abatement efforts also reduce unit damage.

[34]

Interdependencies between the multipliers

There are probably many interdependencies between multipliers of the formulae. Population growth is influenced by growth of output *per capita* and resources *per capita*; productivity of resources is influenced by population growth, and so on. Even without these interdependent influences, population is not a mere multiplier in the economic-environmental relationship, as the standard literature sees it. Population is a participant in the multivariate race with offsetting economic forces. Even if population did not influence these economic forces, population growth could be compensated for by improvements in resource productivity.

The simplest example is livestock which greatly affects water and air quality, and other sanitary conditions. It is well known that the global human population exceeds five billion. It is a less well-known fact that the domesticated animal population of the Earth also exceeds five billion. In 1987, there were over four billion farm animals (think for a moment about almost one billion pigs; or 1·5 billion cows – producing methane by chewing grass!). Their annual average growth rate was about 1 per cent in the 1980s. Growth rate was minus 2·5 per cent in the USA and most market economies and plus 1·3-1·5 per cent in socialist and developing countries (UN Food and Agriculture Organisation, 1988, pp. 241-49). In the Soviet Union, the biological and poisonous waste to water and air from a large collective farm with 108,000 pigs is equal to that of an industrial city with 300,000 people (Lemeshev, 1985, p. 89). A simple calculation shows that improvements in livestock yield in socialist and developing countries towards the levels of Western market economies are capable of compensating for the environmental impact of world population growth. The trade-off between people and pigs or between people and cows may not be a bad deal where the alternative is between people and their standards of living.

De-Industrialisation: Compression of Resources
Over the Production Chains

But how much can productivity of resources increase? Ayres (1978, p. 50) warned against the fallacy that improvements in efficiency of particular processes are limitless. If ferrous scrap constitutes 21-22 per cent of Soviet fabrication of metal products (USSR State Committee on Statistics, 1989, p. 310), and less than that in the United States, where it is recycled anyway, potential improvements are limited indeed. Other material processes seem to have intrinsic chemical limits to input/output productivity. In the USA, only 60 per cent of the dry weight of pulp logs become paper and 40 per cent is residual waste (Haveman, 1974, p. 103). Lovins[1] shows that energy consumption seems to be one area where actual and potential efficiency improvements are large. This is important because the inputs of mineral fuels constituted about 55-56 per cent of the weight of all material inputs in the USA in the 1960s for which extensive data exist.[2] Another area of major improvements in resource productivity and environmental impacts is agriculture, especially livestock production, as can be observed in Tables 6 and 3 and earlier in the text.

The formulae discussed in Appendix A and accumulated evidence open up an additional perspective beyond immediate technological progress in resource processing. It is the compression of producer goods relative to final household goods in market economies. Compression is a descriptive image, not a technical concept. Compression merely describes the reduction of resource-using producer goods in economic processes. This is extremely important because many specific resource outputs are actually inputs in final production. The reduction in input/output ratios compresses the amount of these intermediary outputs over the production processes. Thus an increase in resource productivity transcends into the other multiplier, resource output. The latter is not an independent multiplier in the race with resource productivity. It is also a variable which is itself dependent on resource productivity. Increases in resource productivity extend the race into resource output. There the reduction in input/output ratios continues as the race between producer outputs and final consumer outputs. This means that increases in resource productivity not only outpace increases in resource output but also, eventually, reduce resource output itself. This is the major reason why total resource inputs and pollution decline in Western market economies.

[1] Amory B. Lovins, 'Energy, People, and Industrialization', in Davis and Bernstam (1990).

[2] Kneese, Ayres, d'Arge, 1970, p. 10; corrected in Haveman, 1974, p. 105.

[36]

For example, higher fuel efficiency is achieved by better automotive carburettors. It is also achieved by the elimination of carburettors altogether and the substitution of fuel injection needles. This saves not only more petrol but also steel and aluminium and reduces the stock of machine tools which, in turn, saves steel. There are many 'ripple effects' over the production cycle from such substitutions. Improved livestock breeding is a good example. It increases meat and milk yield per livestock head and leads to a reduction in herd size. This saves feed grains and reduces cultivation, which, in turn, reduces the demand for fertilisers, pesticides, tractors, combines, construction materials, and so on. The reduction of the use of resources extends to petrochemicals, steel, and other fabricated metals. Eventually, improved breeding saves primary metals, ores, and fossil energy. One can consider knock-on effects of improvements in seeds and in the substitution of fibre optics for copper and plastics for metals.

Long-run decline in Western resource consumption
The compression of resources and producer goods over the production processes in the USA and other Western market economies is already apparent. While extensive input/output tables (including the data on net trade in relevant producer and consumer goods) are necessary for documenting this trend, a few simple observations can be made here. Table 5 showed that steel consumption *per capita* declined in the USA and other Western market economies from 1975 to 1985 by about 2 per cent per year. Given low population growth, absolute consumption of steel and its products also declined significantly (US Bureau of the Census, 1989, p. 832). At the same time, production of final consumer goods increased at (or higher than) the rate of real GNP growth (for example, at about 3 per cent per year in the USA). This suggests the phasing-out of many machine tools and other producer goods made from steel.

The USA is a net exporter of both agricultural machinery and grains (US Bureau of the Census, 1989, pp. 787, 793-97). Table 6 shows that the US domestic production of tractors and combines greatly decreased from 1970 to 1987, while grain production increased. Similar simple illustrations concern other industries and products where the output of final household goods

[37]

Table 7

Decadal Indices of Real Gross National Product and Physical Volume of Industrial Production,* USA, 1950 to 1987

	1960/50	1970/60	1980/70	1987/80
Real Gross National Product	1.38	1.45	1.32	1.21
Industrial Production (manufacturing, mining, utilities)	n.a.	n.a.	1.38	1.19
Manufacturing (durable and non-durable goods)	1.44	1.62	1.43**	1.35
Durable Goods	1.43	1.62	1.40	1.22
Primary metals	1.04	1.45	0.95	0.90
Fabricated metal products	1.26	1.51	1.24	1.09
Machinery except electrical	n.a.	1.79	1.69	1.24
Mining	1.21***	1.42	1.13	0.90
Utilities	n.a.	n.a.	1.32	1.03

Notes:
*Federal Reserve Board Series.
**Corrected: the source contains an obvious typographical error.
***1960/1953.
The underlined numbers are at or below the GNP index.

Sources:
GNP, 1950–87 and production, 1970–87: US Bureau of the Census, *Statistical Abstract of the United States, 1989,* Washington, DC: USGPO, 1989, pp. 421, 730.

Production, 1950–70: US Bureau of the Census, *Historical Statistics of the United States, Colonial Times to 1970,* Washington, DC: USGPO, 1975, Pt. 1, p. 585, Pt. 2, p. 667.

increased while the amount of their domestic producer goods increased at a lower rate. At the same time, these producer goods were either exported or their net imports are very recent and small. These producer goods in the USA in the 1970s and the 1980s were, in broad categories, fabricated metal products, machinery (except electrical), and instruments and tools.[1] This simply means that more consumer goods are produced with fewer tools and machines, which reduces resource use and pollution.

Table 7 shows that the growth of the physical volumes of these products consistently declined in the 1960s, the 1970s, and the 1980s. The rate of growth of fabricated metals was lower

[1] For trade data see US Bureau of the Census, 1989, p. 797.

Table 8

Growth of Industrial Production and Real GNP:
Selected Countries and OECD Europe, 1980 to 1987

Index 1980 = 100

	Industrial Production	Real GNP
USA	119	121
Japan	122	129
West Germany	105	111
UK	114	118
France	102	112
Italy	103	114
Netherlands	107	109
Australia	104	124
OECD Europe	108	113

than GNP in the 1970s and the 1980s. Fabricated metals grew slower than overall industrial production, slower than the entire manufacturing sector (which includes both durable and non-durable goods), slower than durable goods in general, and slower than non-electrical machinery. The growth of machinery (except electrical) significantly decelerated and was in the 1980s slower than the entire manufacturing sector. Machinery growth was roughly at the same rate of growth as GNP and durable goods in general. Given that primary metals and fabricated metal products grew even slower, this suggests that many final durable and non-durable consumer products increased faster than their producer goods. These trends in fabricated metals and machinery indicate both a general increase in resource productivity and the compression of producer goods relative to consumer goods. To reiterate, the data are not influenced by changes in imports and exports. Table 7 also shows that the production of primary metals and products of mining underwent absolute decline and that the physical volume of utilities virtually ceased to grow.

A similar overall pattern emerged in the 1980s in most Western market economies. Table 8 compares the indices of the physical volume of industrial production (including manufacturing, mining, and utilities) and real GNP in the largest market economies and in Western Europe as a whole from 1980 to 1987 (OECD, 1989, p. 267; US Bureau of the Census, 1989, p. 823).

Whether these are countries whose economies have a large mining sector (e.g., Australia, UK) or little mining at all (e.g., Japan), whether they are net exporters (e.g., Japan and West Germany) or net importers (e.g., the USA) of manufacturing products, the pattern is the same. In all these countries, the physical volume of industrial production in the 1980s grew slower than in the 1970s and slower than the growth of real GNP.

This and earlier evidence suggests that the compression of resources over the production chains, especially the slowdown in producer goods relative to final consumer goods, is a major factor in declining resource use and diminishing pollution. It can eventually lead to absolute reductions in the total physical volumes of resource-originated outputs, although the *volume* of final consumer goods will increase. If population growth becomes zero or negative, consumer goods and non-resource (i.e. service) outputs may become the only two growing components in market economies.

In the 1980s, a new term emerged in Western vernacular: 'de-industrialisation'. From both economic and environmental perspectives, I do not see anything wrong with this term, nor with the trend associated with it.

3. Cost Minimisation Under Competitive Markets and Input Maximisation Under Regulated State Monopolies

Most readers have probably already deduced from the previous discussion that something akin to the Invisible Environmental Hand is at work in market economies. Competitive firms, in trying to maximise their profits, have to minimise their costs, among other things. They increase productivity via the use of capital stock and energy at early industrial stages when these both substitute for, and are complementary with, labour. However, resources involved in energy conversion, materials processing, and the employment of machinery represent costs. All these costs continue to be minimised. The growth in resource productivity then outpaces the growth of resource output and eventually compresses the producer goods part in the latter. Environmental disruption slows down after the initial rise and then declines at an increasing rate. This result was not a design of participants in open competitive markets. They were driven by profit motives to eventual environmental ends with no intention of their own.

The relationship between economic growth and pollution under competitive markets can also be put in this context. Long-term economic growth is impossible without technological progress. The latter cannot but eventually reduce resource use and environmental discharges. Paradoxically, then, long-term economic growth is impossible without environmental improvements. The Invisible Hand stretches out over two centuries and takes care of this beneficent outcome.

Proliferation of (the Waste of) Resources Over the Production Processes

Under the alternative economic system of regulated socialist monopolies, the proliferation of resources over the production chains never ceases. Figure 1, Tables 5 and 6, and more extensive data in their sources show that, at each level of economic development (approximated as GNP *per capita*), resource use *per capita* and per unit of GNP is significantly higher in socialist than in market economies. Resource use per unit of GNP in socialist countries is about three times as high as in more developed market economies, and resource use *per capita* is either roughly the same in energy or higher in socialist countries in metals and other materials.

A *general comparison* of the production chains in the USA and the Soviet Union can be made. In the second half of the 1980s, consuming about 1·6 times as much steel as the United States, the Soviet Union produced about 0·75-0·80 as much physical volume of metal-originated machinery and other producer goods (Kheinman, 1989, p. 67). With this 75-80 per cent of producer goods, the Soviet Union made less than 33 per cent of final consumer goods relative to the USA (estimated from 40 per cent of GNP *per capita* in the USSR compared with the USA, about 50 per cent share of consumption in the Soviet GNP and 77 per cent in the US GNP, and 18 per cent larger population in the USSR).

The socialist economy can be thought of as a bottom-heavy pyramid with spreading slopes of resources, a gigantic corpus of producer goods and a thin top of final consumer goods. I find it a suggestive coincidence that a roughly estimated overall ratio of

[41]

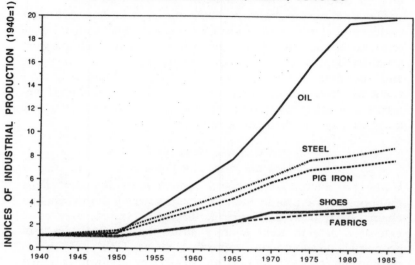

Figure 3
Indices of Industrial Production,
Resources and Final Goods, USSR, 1940-86

Source: USSR State Committee on Statistics, 'Razvitie Promyshlennosti SSSR', *Vestnik Statistiki*, No. 5, 1987, pp. 63-64.

resource inputs to final outputs and the total amount of pollution from stationary sources at the higher bound are both about 4·5-4·8 times higher in the USSR than in the USA (the overall input/output ratio made allowances for the difference in population size and final output *per capita*). The significance of this match of data should be neither exaggerated nor ignored. The data is sketchy and rough, but the above ratio finds additional support in other data provided in this paper and other sources. The numerical comparison fully corresponds to the predictions of the above theory and formulae. (This is consistent with the main thesis of this paper.)

Tables 5 and 6, Figure 1, and other evidence also demonstrate that the divergence in resource use between market and socialist economies has been widening over decades. A major reason is the declining resource productivity and the increasing use of resources in socialist countries. These increases are due to both growing input/output ratios in particular processes and the

Figure 4
Indices of Industrial Production, Resources and
Final Goods, People's Republic of China, 1950-85

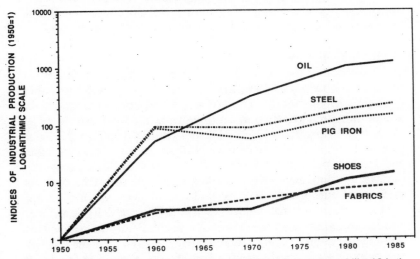

Source: USSR State Committee on Statistics, 'Kitaiskoi Narodnoi Respublike 40 Let', *Vestnik Statistiki*, No. 10, 1989, p. 58.

higher growth of producer goods relative to final consumer goods. Table 6 provides several illustrations of the proliferation of resources or, more precisely, the proliferation of the *waste* of resources over the production chains. The growth of the use of fertilisers, pesticides, and agricultural machinery (with the underlying expansion of metals) relative to grain in the USSR is only one example.

Figures 3 and 4 present evidence for the two largest socialist economies, the Soviet Union and the People's Republic of China, since 1940 and 1950 respectively. In both countries, the gap widened between the production of energy (oil), primary and fabricated metals (pig iron and steel), and final household goods made with the use of resources and producer goods (fabrics and shoes). The trends in production indices are remarkably similar, although the Chinese economy has been fully independent of the Soviet economy since the late 1950s at the latest. This similarity in the proliferation of resources and intermediary inputs over the production chains therefore represents a

[43]

systemic feature. The widening of the gap between the amount of resource inputs and final household outputs over decades cannot be attributed simply to low technological levels. Technology improves over the course of economic development, but this is overpowered by the systemic factors to which I now turn.

'A cannibalistic economy'

To emphasise the growth of producer goods relative to household goods it is necessary to consider, in addition to Table 6, some general trends. The share of final consumer goods in Soviet industrial production declined from 60·5 per cent in 1928 to 39·0 per cent in 1940, to 31·2 per cent in 1950, to 27·5 per cent in 1960, to 26·6 per cent in 1970, to 26·2 per cent in 1980, and to 24·9 per cent in 1987, and the share of producer goods increased accordingly (Kostin, 1989, p. 12). At the same time, as mentioned earlier (above, p. 31), about 33 per cent of the total Soviet industrial production in the 1980s, chiefly producer goods, are considered economically useless outputs, or wastes (Uliukaev, 1989, p. 84; Aganbegian, 1987). In the Soviet economy as a whole, the share of capital investment in the GNP grew in real terms from 24·2 per cent in 1960 to 28·2 per cent in 1970, and to 33·0 per cent in 1980, against about half as much in Western market economies (Ofer, 1987, pp. 1,788, 1,806). This simply means that more machines produce other machines in order to produce other machines which extract additional resources in order to produce more machines. Seliunin (1988, pp. 158-59) called this 'a cannibalistic economy', 'the self-feeding and self-devouring industrialised economy'.

Figure 5 shows where this proliferation of wastes of resources over the production cycle eventually leads. The figure presents Soviet estimates of how much energy it takes and will take to produce energy over the period 1975-2035. In 1975, energy inputs (including energy used to produce equipment for energy extraction) constituted about 22 per cent of energy output of natural gas. This fraction grew to 28 per cent in 1980 and to 32 per cent in 1985 and 1990, and it is projected to increase to 46 per cent in 1995, 58 per cent in 2000 and so on, until it reaches 100 per cent in 2030 and exceeds 100 per cent thereafter. Net energy output grew in absolute terms until 1989 and then began to decline. Absolute declines of gross output are projected after

Figure 5
Gross Output, Energy Input, and Net Output of
Natural Gas Extraction, USSR, 1975-2035
(Reported and Officially Projected)

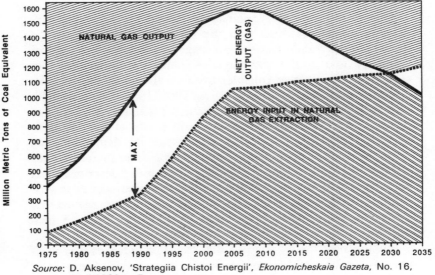

Source: D. Aksenov, 'Strategiia Chistoi Energii', *Ekonomicheskaia Gazeta*, No. 16,
April 1989, p. 5.

Note: Energy from 1 million metric tons of coal equivalent is equal to energy derived
from 789 million cubic metres of natural gas.

2005. Inputs have grown faster than output, and this pattern applies to most economic activities. Furthermore, inputs have grown faster than output at an increasing rate. Eventually, the relationship becomes backward-bending, that is, inputs continue to grow while output declines.

Input Maximisation under Regulated State Monopolies

The remaining question concerns the *causes* of this pattern in socialist economies. I can offer a simple and quick proximate explanation of the proliferation of the waste of resources over the production cycle. At least in the last few decades, supply prices of most outputs have been cost-based and enterprise profits proportional to costs. If one does not believe that enterprise managers are loyal agents of the state but rather that they are individuals who maximise enterprise profits in return for

[45]

managerial bonuses, housing allocations for managers and workers, and other articles of wealth and power, a simple conclusion follows. In order to maximise profits, producers maximise inputs. It pays to maximise costs and wastes over the production processes.[1]

This is a proximate explanation. Readers who find it sufficiently explanatory can skip the rest of this section and go directly to the concluding section (page 51) which offers a global summary and future estimates of pollution under different scenarios. Others may consider the new theory of the socialist economy proposed by Kornai (1979, 1980, 1982, 1986a, 1986b), on which I will draw heavily and which I will also modify. The pre-Kornai literature, from Soviet economists of the 1920s to Western textbooks of the 1980s, emphasises the demander-state in the absence of open competitive markets. The literature does not use this simple concept, however, but rather describes it via such familiar terms as central planning, the command economy, central management, and so on. The demander-state means that the government takes upon itself the determination of production in terms of both quantities and prices.

But the new theory implies that the demander-state is itself only an outcome of the supplier-state. The supplier-state is really at the core of the system in which the government maximises power over individuals via economic means (and also maximises its share of national income and its total revenues via suppressed wages). The supplier-state provides producer firms with inputs (resources, labour, and capital in terms of both money and producer goods) and households with consumer goods. In order to provide, the state must set up producer firms and make them produce. The owner-state and the demander-state follow from this. Another implication is that the supplier-state which wants to maximise its supplier rôle must prevent entry to the market and set up agencies and/or large producer firms that are product monopolies. Indeed, in the Soviet Union in the mid-1980s, the entire industrial production was divided between 46,000 firms (USSR State Committee on Statistics, 1989b, p. 330). Compare this with 1,401,000 industrial establishments with payroll and 2,741,000 tax-paying industrial proprietorships and corporations in the USA (US Bureau of the Census, 1989, pp. 523, 517). In the

[1] See, for example, Gorbachev, 1985, pp. 1-2; Valovoi, 1990, p. 3.

USSR, single corporations controlled by federal agencies produce from 74 to 94 per cent of the volume of particular outputs and the remainder of product markets belongs to local monopolies.[1]

Supplier- and demander-state must feed off itself

Since the supplier-state is also the demander-state, these monopolistic producers are regulated state monopolies on which demand output quotas are imposed. In order to provide, the state has to maintain and expand production of its enterprises, and in order to secure production, the state has to maintain and expand provision of inputs. Thus the state and its own monopolistic firms are locked in a mutually dependent relationship of inputs and outputs. As in any large functioning body, the supplier-state becomes dependent on its own parts.

The five explicit building blocks of Kornai's theory follow from this interdependence and, circularly, from one another. These are, in turn,

o   state subsidisation of corporations or their soft budget constraint;

o   the continuous imposition by selling firms of growing production costs on buying firms;

o   an insatiable demand by enterprises for inputs of money, labour, resources, and producer goods;

o   perpetual shortages of all outputs and inputs combined with price inflation; and

o   the resource constraint on the entire economy.[2]

Once the firms are provided with resources in a way unconstrained by the monetary budget, the state has to increase output of resources and producer goods in order to supply its firms with inputs. Output maximisation becomes the objective function of the supplier-state and the demander-state. The race between inputs and outputs becomes circular.

The tournament between the interdependent state and its

[1] See Kholodkov, 1989; Volkov and Matiukhin, 1989; Nikerov, 1990; Gurevich, 1990; Katsura, 1990.

[2] See also Winiecki, 1983, 1987.

regulated monopolistic firms also becomes circular. Inputs cannot be provided by independent competitive firms since the latter do not exist. Output maximisation makes the supplier-state become more and more dependent on its own producer firms. But these corporations have their own natural interests, they are not loyal agents of the state, and they do not oblige with output maximisation. Their interests are actually opposite to those of the state. The demander-state wishes more output at lower prices and with fewer inputs while monopolistic firms wish to produce less output at higher prices and with more inputs. In the words of Kornai (1986a, p. 55), this is the central issue over which the well-known phenomenon of 'plan bargaining' takes place. Ironically, the poor state, like any other consumer in a monopoly setting, has to succumb to the producer's power and live with both shortages and high prices. Wassily W. Leontief, during his recent trip to the Soviet Union, made a profound unpublished remark. He said that shortages exist not simply due to the excessive demand for, and use of, resources and other products (as Kornai's theory implies), but because there are economic agents interested in creating those shortages.

State monopoly firms raise inputs

As in any other monopoly, the socialist firms raise prices and maximise their rents from output reductions and price-raising, instead of maximising profits from output volume and cost reductions.[1] This alone leads to low productivity of inputs, the failure to adopt advanced technology, and a perpetual excessive use of resources. But the system absorbs inputs much beyond that. Unlike unregulated monopolies in many developing countries, where the government is not responsible for providing inputs and enforcing outputs, socialist regulated monopolies cannot raise prices without the government's consent. They have to bargain with the government, justifying why prices should be raised and output underproduced.

From this follows a missing central point of the Kornai theory. It is the lack of an explanation of why the firms would not economise their inputs. The theory did not explain why the firms are themselves interested in the excessive use of resources, which goes much beyond a mere waste of free or subsidised

[1] See Tullock, 1967; Krueger, 1974; Wenders, 1987.

goods. For, although the enterprises do not have an effective budget constraint, they hit the supply constraint. Resource inputs are always in tight supply. Why, then, do they not use inputs more efficiently?

Doing well by doing badly

The interdependence of the state and the firms and the resulting interdependence of output maximisation and input maximisation provide an explanation. Like a bad and resisting secretary who receives less work from his/her boss than a good secretary, the regulated monopolistic firms are doing well by doing badly. They raise costs, fail to use new technology, waste resources, hoard producer goods, and otherwise maximise inputs in order to justify the cost-based price increases and sabotage the state-imposed demand quotas for output. By maximising inputs, the regulated monopolistic firms exert higher prices and higher profits while producing less. Enterprises effectively show the state how many additional scarce inputs it will take to produce additional output at an even higher price – and the state relaxes the output pressure and pays the price at a mutually agreeable level.

Input maximisation is thus the best profit-maximising behaviour of regulated state monopolies. Cost-based prices and cost-proportional profits which directly create input maximisation have emerged in the interests of state monopolistic producers. This does not mean that the government is myopic, let alone blind, in allowing and even inviting these input maximising arrangements. Far from it; the government is fully aware that its producer firms will raise prices, reduce output, and maximise inputs as a means to achieve these aims. Cost-based prices and cost-proportional profits are then in the interest of the government as much as they are in the interests of corporations. These are government monitoring devices which provide negotiating ground where input-output and input-price agreements are reached between the demander-state and producers. Kornai (1986a, p. VIII) pointed out that some socialist arrangements are reminiscent of Western military industries. I relegate to Appendix B (below, pp. 63-65) a more detailed and technical discussion of input maximisation.

[49]

Maximising inputs as the end-result

Input maximisation at the enterprise level leads to the main paradox of the socialist economic system. The supplier-state strives for output maximisation but its own producer firms maximise profits via input maximisation. Since the state economy is simply an aggregation of its producer firms over the production cycle, the entire system adopts the mode of input maximisation. *The state actually maximises the production of inputs under the appearance of the maximisation of output.* As long as economic growth continues and the government collects revenues via suppressed wages and residual enterprise profits (after subtracting management bonuses, housing and other direct allocations to enterprises, etc.), the government is content. It is when input maximisation eventually impedes economic growth and inputs exceed outputs that the government revolts against its own system.

The Special Function of the Waste of Resources in Input Maximisation

In the tournament between the demander-state and its monopolistic producer firms, inputs of physical resources become a special weapon. Enterprises deliberately waste them in order to make the costs of additional production prohibitively steep for the government. Consider that producers make life difficult for the demanding government, not for their buying firms or consumers. The commercial buyers – that is, other corporations – are willing to pay higher prices for additional output because they pass their costs via higher prices onto their own buyers on the next stage of the production chains. Consumers are also willing to pay, given the shortages – at least some are, because demand is price inelastic, as Appendix B illustrates. The pressure of all these buyers on the government for inputs and/or outputs is transmitted by the state to the producers of inputs. The pressure is circular over the production chains. Collusion between firms for reducing demand pressures is not often feasible because few producers form a mutual input-output cycle.

Resource inputs and producer goods, unlike monetary inputs, are a physical constraint, and even the all-owning government cannot give more than it has. Therefore, maximisation of resources, of all inputs, is the optimal means for producers to raise prices and reduce the demand output quotas. High input/ output ratios and outright waste of resources and producer goods in production processes is the optimal means to increase profits. Socialist enterprises are interested in the waste of resources. In the Soviet Union, each five-year plan since the 1950s dictated final consumer goods to grow relative to producer goods and each five-year period of actual economic performance ended the other way around. This is one of the fall-outs of the system which the government could never control and has long since given up trying.

4. Which Path of Economic Development?

If economic systems influence environmental conditions more than do levels of GNP *per capita*, then the global environmental future depends in large part on the choice of economic system in developing countries. This is simply because developing and newly industrialised countries constitute more than three-quarters of the world population. As their GNP *per capita* grows, the resource use *per capita* and the discharges of polluting residuals *per capita* are likely to lie between the extreme parameters typical for one or another system. This section will provide a global summary of the relationship between economic growth and resource use (and the implied pollution) *per capita*. Then it will present estimates of the parameters of pollution broken down by economic systems and offer several scenarios for the future of the global environment depending on the prevailing choice of economic system.

Table 9 and Figure 6 summarise the long-term relationship between GNP *per capita* and energy use *per capita*, given the economic system. It has been shown that trends in environmental damage closely correspond to trends in resource use *per capita*; that energy use constitutes about one-half of total resource use; and that trends in energy use and total resource use *per capita* by economic systems are very close over time. Hence, in the absence of other data of similar scope, the energy analysis in Table 9 and Figure 6 should be representative of the long-term trends in overall resource use and pollution *per capita* by economic systems.

[*Contd. on p. 54*]

[51]

Table 9

Regressions of Energy–GNP and Energy–Population Relationships across Nations, 1982

Equation Number	1	2	3	4
Dependent Variables	Energy Consumption per Capita			Total Energy Consumption
Independent Variables				
Constant	−0.56** (2.96)	−1.48** (9.75)	−1.42** (5.58)	−5.52** (2.98)
GNP per Capita	1.56** (5.97)	1.70** (8.85)	1.40** (3.09)	2.35** (3.94)
GNP-per-Capita Squared	−0.45** (2.72)	−0.64** (4.86)	−0.44* (1.67)	−0.99** (3.02)
US and Canada		0.97** (12.54)	1.25** (5.44)	2.98 (1.54)
Statism	0.46** (3.75)	0.45** (4.33)	0.25** (2.26)	0.98** (2.68)
Industry			0.46** (2.64)	
Service			−0.50* (1.68)	
Population Size				2.05** (2.96)
Population Size Squared				−0.85** (2.78)
$\bar{R}^2$	0.74	0.86	0.89	0.66
F-statistic	47.36	75.63	45.77	16.86
No. of countries	49	49	33	49

Notes: All estimates are heteroskedastic-consistent.
t-statistics are in parentheses.
**Significant at 1% level.
* Significant at 5% level.

Data source: Margaret E. Slade, 'Natural Resources, Population Growth, and Economic Well-Being', in D. Gale Johnson and Ronald D. Lee (eds), *Population Growth and Economic Development: Issues and Evidence*, Madison, WI: University of Wisconsin Press, 1987, p. 355. (All estimates are mine.)

Commentary on Table 9

There are four nested ordinary least squares regressions. The functional form is linear but I equalised the means so that coefficients represent elasticities. I added to Slade's tests a dummy variable called 'statism' for socialist countries, both developed and developing (e.g., China, Cuba, Ethiopia), but not for Yugoslavia, because enterprises are more independent from the demander-state in Yugoslavia, and therefore do not need to practice input maximisation.

In the first three equations, energy consumption *per capita* is regressed on GNP *per capita*, the quadratic term of GNP *per capita*, the type of economic system, and some other variables. Among them, Equation 3 includes the shares of the labour force in industry and services. Resource use *per capita* is predicted to have a positive relationship with the former and a negative one with the latter. The number of observations is reduced in this equation due to lack of data.

The quadratic form of GNP *per capita* is added to the set of exogenous variables in all equations for the following reason. The predicted sign of the GNP-energy relationship in the overall sample of 49 developed market, developed socialist, and various developing countries is positive. But the prediction is that the long-term relationship becomes negative in market economies and that the earlier positive relationship gradually lowers its slope over the course of economic growth. The quadratic form of GNP *per capita* tests the prediction that resource use per capita increases at a decreasing rate and then declines – that is, the predicted sign of the coefficient of the GNP-per-capita squared is negative. This prediction means that the growth of the economy, as opposed to the level of GNP *per capita*, is negatively related to resource use *per capita*.

The fourth equation regresses total energy consumption on the same set of variables plus population size and the quadratic form of population size. The rationale for the latter is similar to using the quadratic form of GNP *per capita*. Following Slade (1987), a dummy variable for the USA and Canada (where *per capita* use of energy is higher than in other countries) was added in three of the four equations. This sharpens the performance of regressions but does not change the nature of the findings (compare Equations 1 and 2).

All the coefficients in all four equations have predicted signs and are statistically significant at the 1 per cent or 5 per cent levels. The tests show that the currently prevailing relationship between resource use *per capita* and GNP *per capita* is positive but that the overall shape of this relationship is non-linear. The shape of the curve is non-monotonically concave and decreasing: that is, as GNP *per capita* grows, resource use *per capita* decelerates and then declines. Interestingly, the relationship between population size and resource use has the same shape. The industrial share of the economy is positively and the share of services is negatively related to resource use *per capita* at each given level of GNP *per capita*. The principal finding is the rôle of 'statism'. It is positively and statistically significantly related to resource use in all four equations.

Following and modifying the original tests by Slade (1987, pp. 353-56), Table 9 analyses the relationship between GNP *per capita* and energy use *per capita* in 1982 in 49 countries with different economic systems. Readers interested in the econometric discussion are referred to the commentary in the Box accompanying Table 9 (pp. 52-53).

Figure 6 depicts the actual shapes of the relationships between energy use *per capita* and GNP *per capita* in 1982 for the subsamples of market and socialist economies. The data are combined from Slade (1987, p. 355), Winiecki (1987, p. 25), and Tables 5 and 9. Figure 6 thus effectively summarises the ideas and evidence of this paper. It shows the split in the trends in resource use over the course of economic growth between market and socialist economies. In competitive market countries, the relationship between GNP *per capita* and resource use is initially positive; resource use increases at a decreasing rate in response to economic growth, until the level of development achieved some time in the 1970s turns the relationship into an increasingly negative one. In socialist countries, resource use *per capita* grows continuously over the course of economic growth and even after the economies begin to decline. Eventually, in accordance with Figure 5, resource use may decline as the economies decline further. The curve thus becomes backward bending.

As I suggested above, the non-monotonically concave and decreasing curve in market economies applies also to the long-term trends in pollution: over the course of their economic growth, pollution first increases at a decreasing rate and then declines. The case of socialist economies was more simple (that is, an ever-increasing pollution with or without economic growth), until economic crisis prompted both economic reforms and environmental actions.

Future Economic Scenarios and Projected Global Pollution

Table 10 summarises the range of the current state of emissions of traditional air pollutants by three groups of economies. Emissions include carbon monoxide, sulphur oxide, nitrogen oxide, particulate matter, volatile organic compounds, and lead. Table 10 also projects the increases in global pollution under different scenarios. That is, how many times will the *per capita*

[54]

Figure 6
Relationship Between Energy Use Per Capita and GNP Per Capita Under Different Economic Systems

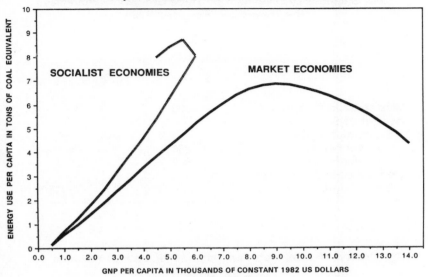

Source: Derived from Jan Winiecki, *Economic Prospects – East and West*, London: The Centre for Research into Communist Economies, 1987, p. 25; and from Figure 1 and Tables 5 and 9 and their sources.

amount of emissions increase if one or another of the current systems of production is adopted by the entire world. These estimates and projections are necessarily as tentative and rough as the current state of ignorance will allow. This is especially true for developed socialist countries, for which this paper is the first attempt to estimate the lower and higher bounds of overall air pollution as discussed above. For less developed and newly industrialised countries, which constitute over three-quarters of the world population, estimates of international agencies are taken as the lower bound. These agencies imply that about 100 MMT of air pollutants are emitted per year in this part of the world. Since this number cannot be verified, I put in parentheses some estimates of what may happen if the true number is twice as high. These parentheses do not imply a preference for one or another bound.

[55]

Table 10

Estimates of Emissions of Air Pollutants in Relation to Population and Economic Development by Three Groups of Economies: by Three Scenarios, *circa* 1986

Panel A

Emissions of Air Pollutants

	Per Capita (kilograms)	Per $1,000 of GNP (kilograms)
Western Market Economies	350	30
Developed Socialist Economies (DSEs)		
Lower bound	350	75
Higher bound	800	175
Less Developed and Newly Industrialised Countries	50 (100)	75 (150)

Panel B

Proportion of World's Population, GNP, and Air Pollution
(*per cent*)

	Population	GNP	Air Pollution Lower bound for DSEs	Air Pollution Higher bound for DSEs
Western Market Economies	15.2	68.9	45.0	35.0 (28.0)
Developed Socialist Economies	7.5	13.7	22.3	40.0 (32.0)
Less Developed and Newly Industrialised Countries	77.3	17.4	32.7	25.0 (40.0)

Conventional categories obscure more than they reveal

The conventional division by three categories of countries in Table 10 and elsewhere in this paper is not very illuminating. The category of the less developed and newly industrialised countries (often misleadingly lumped together as 'developing countries') combines economies which are vastly different in their level of GNP *per capita* and economic systems. In fact, many newly industrialised countries have higher GNP *per capita* than developed socialist countries. The current averages of pollution

[56]

Table 10 continued   Panel C

If the entire world assumes the parameters of a given economic
setting, global emission of air pollutants would multiply
as follows:

	Multiplier for global pollution: per capita	per $1,000 of GNP
With the parameters of:		
Western Market Economies		
Lower bound for DSEs	3.0	0.65
Higher bound for DSEs	2.3 (1.9)	0.50 (0.41)
Developed Socialist Economies		
Lower bound for DSEs	3.0	1.63
Higher bound for DSEs	5.3 (4.3)	2.92 (2.34)
Less Developed and Newly Industrialised Countries		
Lower bound for DSEs	0.4	1.88
Higher bound for DSEs	0.3 (0.5)	1.44 (2.30)

Sources:
   Population and GNP: Calculated from The World Bank, *World Development Report,
1988,* New York: Oxford University Press, 1988, pp. 187, 222–23. The average GNP *per
capita* in developed socialist countries in 1986 is estimated at $5,200, i.e., 40% of that
in Western market economies.
   Emission of Air Pollutants: Calculated from OECD, *OECD Environmental Data
Compendium, 1989,* Paris: OECD, 1989, pp. 17–19. Pollution in socialist economies is
estimated by the author. See Sections 1 and 4 of the text for discussion of estimates.

Notes:
   The lower bound assumes a 77% rate of success in abatement of air pollution from
stationary sources in developed socialist economies. The higher bound assumes a 30%
rate.
   The numbers in parentheses refer to higher pollution estimates for less developed
countries. Note that the *OECD Environmental Data Compendium* implies the amount
of polluting discharges in all less developed and newly industrialised countries as about
100 million metric tons per year. This amount is almost certainly underestimated.
Doubling the amount of discharges per $1,000 of GNP and *per capita* in these countries
in Panel A would alter the multipliers in Panel C. For the higher bound for DSEs, global
pollution would increase 1.9 times under global market economies, 4.3 times under
global socialist economies and 0.5 times under global adoption of current economic
parameters (including the standard of living) of less developed countries.

per capita for the third category are presented here only because
the newly industrialised countries constitute a small fraction of
the population of the 'developing' world. The averages are thus
not significantly biased downward. After all these admissions of
ignorance and caveats, the estimates in Table 10 have only two
justifications: they seem to lie within possible ranges and are
better than nothing.

   It can be calculated from Panel A of Table 10 that in 1986 the
total amount of global emissions of air pollutants was 577 MMT

[57]

if pollution in both socialist and developing countries is calculated at their respective lower bounds. Global pollution was 742 MMT at the higher bound for socialist and at the lower bound for developing countries. And it was 932 MMT at the higher bound for both these groups. On a *per capita* basis, pollution was 350 kg in market countries, from 350 kg to 800 kg in developed socialist countries (DSEs), and from 50 to 100 kg in less developed and newly industrialised countries. Interestingly, at both lower and higher bounds, pollution per $1,000 of GNP was roughly the same in DSEs and developing countries. This alone shows that the higher technological level in DSEs could not overpower the systemic impact of input maximisation and deliberately wasteful practices in resource use.

Panel B shows that Western market economies produce a smaller fraction of global pollution than their share of global GNP while socialist countries produce a higher fraction. Both, of course, produce a higher fraction of world pollution than their share of world population. At the higher bound of pollution estimates, socialist countries produce a higher share of global pollution (from 32 to 40 per cent) than Western market economies, although the latter have twice as high a share of world population and five times as high a share of global GNP.

Panel C provides multipliers of global pollution increases under different scenarios. These multipliers do not take into account future population growth because estimates are made only per $1,000 of GNP and *per capita*. Also, they project future pollution *per capita* in terms of global averages. This actually means that only the areas with lower pollution than the chosen standard will increase environmental disruption, much of which will be local. Panel C shows that in the unlikely case of the entire world moving to the levels of GNP *per capita* and pollution *per capita* of the average developing country, global pollution *per capita* will decline from one-third to one-half of its present level. Given world population growth, present total amounts of emissions will not decline much under this scenario, and the total economic sacrifice may not be worth considering even from the extreme environmental standpoint.

The worst possible range of future pollution provides the global socialist scenario. Environmental damage will increase from 3·0 to 5·3 times *per capita* under global transition to socialist

[58]

economic parameters, and twice that much given world population growth. The scenario of global economic development along the lines of Western market economies promises increases of air pollution *per capita* in the world from 1·9 to 3·0 times. Again, increases will be additionally twice as high given world population growth. This scenario may significantly improve if the present trends in the reduction of pollution continue and accelerate over the course of economic growth in market economies. To conclude, *the future of world environmental conditions depends to a significant extent on the choice of economic system in developing countries.*

5. Conclusions

Since economic development of currently less developed countries will increase local and global pollution under any conceivable scenario, two compensatory factors acquire special significance. One is the economic transition from regulated state monopolies to open competitive markets in socialist countries, especially in the USSR and China. The other is continuous economic growth in Western market economies. Both these developments will be accompanied by major, continuous, and accelerating increases in resource productivity and reductions in resource use and pollution. These two compensatory factors may be large enough to offset global (but not local) impacts of economic development in less developed countries.

These conclusions are either paradoxical or plain wrong from the standpoint of the standard literature. They are correct if the race between population growth and resource productivity is the driving force of economic development and if resource productivity is winning in the long term under market economies. At the least, these conclusions offer some viable perspective for the world by reconciling economic development and the environment. And what do standard literature and standard policies offer for the world? – merely economic stagnation and elaborate international controls. Economic growth under open competitive markets offers a better choice for both the economy and the environment.

[59]

APPENDIX A
Resource Productivity in the Algebraic Identities of Environmental Damage

The law of conservation of mass is satisfied when the total amount of resource inputs and the total amount of resource-using outputs are included for measuring environmental damage. While constructing these total amounts, I separate industrial production and household wastes. The quantity of the latter is not dependent on technological progress, although its unit damage may be. In addition, my approach disaggregates individual resources and individual countries. This allows us to capture major damages embodied in small quantities of some discharges and to avoid the problem of aggregation. Total environmental damage can be measured as:

$$\dot{D} = \sum_{1}^{N} P_i \left[\left(\sum_{0}^{J} R_{ji}^{P} d_{ji}^{R} \right) + H_i^{P} d_i^{H} \right] \quad , \quad (1)$$

$$i = 1, 2, \ldots, N \quad j = 1, 2, \ldots, J$$

$$\dot{D} = \sum_{1}^{N} P_i \left\{ \left[\sum_{0}^{J} \left(0_{ji}^{P} + W_{ji}^{P} \right) d_{ji}^{0,W} \right] + H_i^{P} d_i^{H} \right\} \quad , \quad (2)$$

$$i = 1, 2, \ldots, N \quad j = 1, 2, \ldots, J$$

and

$$\dot{D} = \sum_{1}^{N} P_i \left[\left(\sum_{0}^{J} 0_{ji}^{P} R_{ji}^{0} d_{ji}^{R} \right) + H_i^{P} d_i^{H} \right] \quad , \quad (3)$$

$$i = 1, 2, \ldots, N \quad j = 1, 2, \ldots, J$$

where D is the total flow of environmental damages from processing of all resources j in all countries i. P_i is population of each country i. R_{ji}^P represents resource inputs *per capita* for each resource j in each country i. O_{ji}^P is economic (useful) output *per capita* originated in each resource j in each country i; and W_{ji}^P is economic waste *per capita* for j and i. H_i^P is household waste *per capita* in each country. One can define this as biological waste only, or also include trash and recreational waste; if not included in household waste, the latter two must be included in O_i^P and W_i^j as their used-up residuals. $d_{ji}^{O,W}$ is environmental damage per unit of resource-originated output, both economic and wasteful, in each j and i. d_{ji}^R is damage per unit of mass of j's resource input processing over the production chains in i's country. d_i^H is a similar damage measure of household waste. R_{ji}^O in Equation 3 is the total input/useful output ratio. This is the inverse of the productivity of resources. By definition,

$$R_{ji}^O = R_{ji}^P / O_{ji}^P.$$

The right-hand sides of Equations (1) and (2) are equal by the law of conservation of mass and by the identity of the total environmental damage. The proof of Equation (3) is trivial. It simply modifies the term for resource inputs in Equation (1) as the product of useful output and the input/useful output ratio.

APPENDIX B
A Model of Input Maximisation

Figure A1 shows two combinations of quantities and prices on an inelastic demand curve DD. These two combinations reproduce the rent-seeking model of Tullock (1967; see elaboration in Wenders, 1987). Once product monopoly is obtained and the supply is inelastic in the absence of competitive markets, the demand also becomes inelastic. On an inelastic (vertically sloped) demand curve, it is more gainful for a monopolistic producer to sell the quantity Q_R at the price P_R than the quantity Q_C at the price P_C. The associated parallelograms drawn with broken and straight lines, respectively, show this result.

If the monopoly is unregulated, there is no need to increase production costs. Higher prices can be charged and rents extracted subject to the demand curve and the highest profitable combination of prices and quantities, irrespective of costs. These unit costs are shown on the marginal costs curve MC. Even in the absence of competition and downward price pressures, it is profitable for producers to reduce marginal costs, although they do not have as strong incentives to do this as under competitive markets. But if the monopoly is state-owned and regulated and the tournament takes place between the government and the producer over the combination of prices and quantities, the rules of the game are different.

In order to reduce quantities to Q_R and raise prices to P_R, and to justify this most profitable combination, the regulated monopolistic firms have to uplift and reshape their marginal costs curves. The government has to face the impossibility of additional production beyond the point Q_R unless the demand curve is moved outward, capacity is increased, supplies of inputs are increased, and prices even higher than P_R are paid. Since the demander-state is simultaneously the supplier-state, the given

[63]

Figure A1
Rent-Seeking and Input Maximisation Under Unregulated and Regulated Monopolies

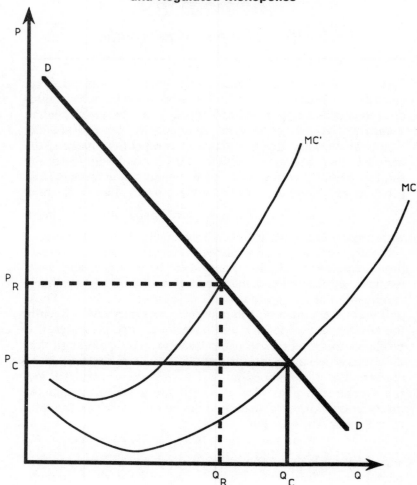

demand curve signifies also the supply constraints of inputs (not only money, but also labour, capacity, resources, and producer goods). Raising production costs under the supplier-state means demanding more inputs. The uplifting of the marginal costs curve from MC to MC' by monopolistic producers puts the government on the edge. The combination of P_R and Q_R has to be accepted. The above logic also suggests that the new marginal costs curve MC' has to be steeper than MC.

Alternatively, the government has to enforce lower marginal costs. This can be done either by terrorising enterprise management, or by using forced labour with few producer goods, or by confiscating output at nominal prices and not providing inputs. The third option is most suitable for agriculture where people have to produce for their own subsistence and where both subsistence output and inputs of seed and feed grains can be confiscated in lieu of saleable outputs. This option, however, cannot be repeated for long and does not provide for necessary expansion of the supplier-state. The second option is low productive and the first option was rejected by the managerial class when it became more powerful. The uplifting of marginal costs curves then becomes the prevailing and winning game.

One needs to emphasise that under the supplier-state, raising production costs from MC to MC' means predominantly increasing physical inputs of resources and producer goods. These are the inputs whose maximisation is the most powerful weapon for enterprises against the supplier-state. Input maximisation is circular over the production cycle and is ever-growing. The supplier-state has to demand outputs that become inputs which are being maximised. This game of output maximisation and input maximisation is repeated over and over again, until the system cannot sustain itself.

[65]

Bibliography

Aganbegian, Abel G. (1987): 'Otstupat nekuda', *Izvestiia*, 25 August, p. 2.

Ayres, Robert U. (1978): *Resources, Environment, and Economics: Applications of the Materials/Energy Balance Principle*, New York: John Wiley and Sons.

——, and Allen V. Kneese (1969): 'Production, Consumption and Externalities,' *The American Economic Review*, Vol. 59, No. 2, pp. 282-97.

Baumol, William J., and Wallace E. Oates, 'Long-run Trends in Environmental Quality', in Julian L. Simon and Herman Kahn (eds.), *The Resourceful Earth: A Response to Global 2000*, Oxford: Basil Blackwell, pp. 439-75.

Davis, Kingsley (1986): 'Low Fertility in Evolutionary Perspective', *Population and Development Review*, Supplement to Vol. 12, pp. 48-65.

——, and Mikhail S. Bernstam (eds.) (1990): *Resources, Environment, and Population: Present Knowledge, Future Options*, Supplement to *Population and Development Review*, Vol. 16.

Forsund, Finn R. (1985): 'Input-Output Models, National Economic Models, and the Environment', in Allen V. Kneese and James L. Sweeney (eds.), *Handbook of Natural Resource and Energy Economics*, Vol. 1, Amsterdam: North-Holland, pp. 325-41.

Gorbachev, M. S. (1985): 'O Sozyve Ocherednogo XXVII Sezda KPSS i Zadachakh Po Ego Podgotovke i Organizatsii', *Pravda*, 24 April, pp. 1-5.

Gzovskii, V. (1985): 'Sotsialnye Problemy Okhrany Okruzhaiushchei Sredy v Stranakh SEV', *Voprosy Ekonomiki*, No. 12, pp. 99-108.

Gurevich, V. (1990): 'Tupiki Totalnogo Monopolizma', *Ekonomika i Zhizn*, No. 13, p. 5.

[67]

Haveman, Robert H. (1974): 'On Estimating Environmental Damage: A Survey of Recent Research in the United States', in *Environmental Damage Costs*, Paris: OECD, pp. 101-31.

Holdern, John P., and Paul R. Ehrlich (1974): 'Human Population and the Global Environment', *American Scientist*, Vol. 62, pp. 282-92.

Hufschmidt, Maynard M., David E. James, Anton D. Meisner, Blair T. Bower, and John A. Dixon (eds.) (1983): *Environment, Natural Systems and Development: An Economic Valuation Guide*, Baltimore, MD: Johns Hopkins University Press.

Iablokov, A. (1989): 'Spasenie Prirody i Zakon', *Izvestiia*, 8 October, p. 2.

Illarionov, A. (1990): 'Paradoksy Statistiki', *Argumenty i Fakty*, No. 3, pp. 6-7.

James, David (1985): 'Environmental Economics, Industrial Process Models and Regional-Residuals Management Models', in Allen V. Kneese and James L. Sweeney (eds.), *Handbook of Natural Resource and Energy Economics*, Vol. 1, Amsterdam: North-Holland, pp. 271-324.

Katsura, P. M. (1990): 'Kak Poborot Monopolizm', *Izvestiia*, 3 March, p. 2.

Kheinman, S. (1989): 'O Problemakh Nauchno-Tekhnicheskoi politiki', *Voprosy Ekonomiki*, No. 3, pp. 65-74.

Kholodkov, V. (1989): 'Diktat Proizvoditelia i Rynok', *Ekonomicheskaia Gazeta*, No. 22, p. 16.

Kneese, Allen V. (1977): *Economics and the Environment*, New York: Penguin Books.

———, Robert U. Ayres, Ralph C. d'Arge (1970): *Economics and the Environment: A Materials Balance Approach*, Baltimore, MD: The Johns Hopkins Press for Resources for the Future, Inc.

Kornai, Janos (1979): 'Resource-Constrained versus Demand-Constrained Systems', *Econometrica*, Vol. 47, No. 4, July, pp. 801-19.

[68]

—— (1980): *Economics of Shortage*, Vols. 1-2, Amsterdam: North-Holland.

—— (1982): *Growth, Shortage and Efficiency: A Macrodynamic Model of the Socialist Economy*, Berkeley: University of California Press.

—— (1986a): *Contradictions and Dilemmas: Studies on the Socialist Economy and Society*, Cambridge, MA: MIT Press.

—— (1986b): 'The Hungarian Reform Process: Visions, Hopes, and Reality', *Journal of Economic Literature*, Vol. 24, No. 2, pp. 1,687-1,737.

Kostin, L. (1989): 'Litsom k Cheloveku', *Agitator*, No. 15, pp. 12-15.

Krueger, Anne (1974): 'The Political Economy of the Rent-Seeking Society', *The American Economic Review*, Vol. 64, No. 3, June, pp. 291-303.

Lemeshev, M. Ia. (1985): 'Prodovolstvennaia Programma i Okhrana Okruzhaiushchei Sredy', *Voprosy Ekonomiki*, No. 12, pp. 79-89.

Lisovenko, N., and V. Trach (1989): 'Protivogaz Dlia Goroda', *Izvestiia*, 5 October, p. 3.

Lukianenko, V. (1989): 'Drama Vody', *Pravda*, 11 August, p. 2.

Nikerov, G. (1990): 'Ot Gigantomanii k Konkurentsii', *Argumenty i Fakty*, No. 1, p. 2.

OECD (1989): *OECD Environmental Data Compendium 1989*, Paris: OECD.

Ofer, Gur. (1987): 'Soviet Economic Growth: 1928-1985', *The Journal of Economic Literature*, Vol. 25, No. 4, December, pp. 1,767-1,833.

Rimashevskaia, N. M. (1990): 'Uzlovaia Problema Perekhodnogo Perioda', *Voprosy Ekonomiki*, No. 1, pp. 33-36.

Samsonov, E. (1989): 'Tsena Zemli', *Pravitelstvennyi Vestnik*, No. 19, p. 11.

Seliunin, Vasilii (1988): 'Glubokaia Reforma ili Revansh Biurokratii?', *Znamia*, No. 7, pp. 155-67.

[69]

Simon, Julian L. (1981): *The Ultimate Resource*, Princeton, NJ: Princeton University Press.

Simons, Marlise (1990): 'Pollution's Toll in Eastern Europe: Stumps Where Great Trees Once Grew', *The New York Times*, 19 March, p. 9.

Slade, Margaret E. (1987): 'Natural Resources, Population Growth and Economic Well-Being', in D. Gale Johnson and Ronald D. Lee (eds.), *Population Growth and Economic Development: Issues and Evidence*, Madison: The University of Wisconsin Press, pp. 331-69.

Smil, Vaclav (1984): *The Bad Earth: Environmental Degradation in China*, New York: Sharpe.

———, and T. Kuz (1976): 'A New Look at Energy and GDP Correlation', *Energy International*, Vol. 13, No. 1, pp. 31-34.

Tsaturov, Iu. S. (1989): 'Kto Dast Nam Shans', *Nedelia*, No. 33, p. 13.

Tullock, Gordon (1967): 'The Welfare Costs of Tariffs, Monopolies and Theft', *Western Economic Journal*, Vol. 5, No. 2, June, pp. 224-32.

Uliukaev, A. (1989): 'Novaia Istoriia Gammelnskogo Dudochnika', *Kommunist*, No. 18, pp. 78-86.

United Nations Environment Programme (1987): *Environmental Data Report*, Oxford: Basil Blackwell.

UN Food and Agriculture Organisation (1988): *FAO Yearbook, Production, 1987*, Vol. 41, Rome: UNFAO.

US Bureau of the Census (1989): *Statistical Abstract of the United States, 1989*, Washington DC: US Government Printing Office.

US Commission on Population Growth and the American Future (1972): Ronald G. Ridker (ed.), *Population, Resources, and the Environment*, Vol. 3, Washington DC: USGPO.

US President (1987): *Economic Report of the President, 1987*, Washington DC: USGPO.

USSR State Committee on Statistics (1989a): *Okhrana*

IEA PUBLICATIONS
Subscription Service

An annual subscription is the most convenient way to obtain our publications. Every title we produce in all our regular series will be sent to you immediately on publication and without further charge, representing a substantial saving.

Individual subscription rates*

Britain: £30·00 p.a. including postage.
£28·00 p.a. if paid by Banker's Order.
£18·00 p.a. to teachers and students who pay *personally*.

Europe: £30·00 p.a. including postage.

South America: £40·00 p.a. or equivalent.

Other Countries: Rates on application. In most countries subscriptions are handled by local agents. Addresses are available from the IEA.

* These rates are *not* available to companies or to institutions.

To: The Treasurer, Institute of Economic Affairs,
2 Lord North Street, Westminster,
London SW1P 3LB

I should like to subscribe from ....

I enclose a cheque/postal order for:

☐ £30·00

☐ £18·00   I am a teacher/student at ....
....

☐ Please send a Banker's Order form.
☐ Please send an invoice.
☐ Please charge my credit card:

Please tick   ☐ 𝘝𝘐𝘚𝘈   ☐ ▲   ☐ AMERICAN EXPRESS   ☐ ◑

Card No: ☐☐☐☐☐☐☐☐☐☐☐☐☐☐☐☐☐☐

In addition I would like to purchase the following previously published titles:

....
....

Name ....

Address ....

....   } BLOCK LETTERS PLEASE

.... Post Code ....

Signed .... Date ....

OP85

Okruzhaiushchei Sredy i Ratsionalnoe Ispolzovanie Prirodnykh Resursov SSSR, Moscow: Finansy i Statistika.

—— (1989b): *Narodnoe Khoziaistvo SSSR v 1988 Godu. Statisticheskii Ezhegodnik,* Moscow: Finansy i Statistika.

—— (1989c): 'Selskoe Khoziaistvo', *Politicheskoe Obrazovanie,* No. 6, pp. 13-14.

USSR Supreme Soviet (1989): 'O Neotlozhnykh Merakh Ekologicheskogo Obnovleniia Strany', *Pravda,* 3 December, pp. 1-2.

Valentei, A. (1990): 'Ob Ekologii Bez Prikras', *Ekonomika i Zhizn,* No. 3, p. 24.

Valovoi, D. (1990): 'Plata Za Rastochitelstvo', *Pravda,* 2 March, p. 3.

Volkov, N. and G. Matiukhin (1989): 'Konkurentsiia i Monopolii', *Pravda,* 29 June, p. 4.

Voloshin, V. (1990): 'Kakuiu Vodu My Piem', *Okhrana Truda i Sotsialnoe Strakhovanie,* No. 1, pp. 2-7.

Wenders, John T. (1987): 'On Perfect Rent Dissipation', *The American Economic Review,* Vol. 77, No. 3, June, pp. 456-59.

Winiecki, Jan (1983): 'Resource Constraints and East European Foreign Trade Structures', *Intereconomics: Review of International Trade and Development,* Vol. 18, No. 3, pp. 125-29.

—— (1987): *Economic Prospects – East and West,* London: The Centre for Research into Communist Economies.

The World Bank (1988): *World Development Report, 1988,* New York: Oxford University Press.

Yoichi, Kaya, Yamaji Kenju, and Matsuhashi Ryuji, 'A Grand Strategy for Global Warming', Paper presented at the Tokyo Conference on Global Environment, September 1989.